Spanish
Phrases
FOR
DUMMIES®

by Susana Wald

Wiley Publishing, Inc.

Spanish Phrases For Dummies®

Published by
Wiley Publishing, Inc.
111 River St.
Hoboken, NJ 07030-5774
www.wiley.com

For general information on our other products and services or to obtain technical support, please contact our Customer Care Department within the U.S. at 800-762-2974, outside the U.S. at 317-572-3993, or fax 317-572-4002.

Wiley also publishes its books in a variety of electronic formats. Some content that appears in print may not be available in electronic books.

Library of Congress Control Number: 2004107388.

ISBN: 0-7645-7204-0

Manufactured in the United States of America

10 9 8 7 6 5 4 3 2 1

1B/QS/QX/QU/IN

About the Author

Susana Wald is a writer and simultaneous and literary translator in Hungarian, Spanish, English, and French. As a publisher, she has been working with books and authors for many years. She has been a teacher in Chile and in Canada and has known the joy of learning from her students and their untiring enthusiasm and tolerance. She also is an artist and has had her work shown in many countries in Europe and in North, Central, and South America.

Publisher's Acknowledgments

We're proud of this book; please send us your comments through our Dummies online registration form located at www.dummies.com/register/.

Some of the people who helped bring this book to market include the following:

Acquisitions, Editorial, and Media Development

Compiler: Laura Peterson

Senior Project Editor: Tim Gallan

Acquisitions Editor: Stacy Kennedy

Copy Editors: Laura K. Miller, E. Neil Johnson

Assistant Editor: Holly Gastineau-Grimes

Technical Editor: Language Training Center

Editorial Manager: Christine Meloy Beck

Editorial Assistant: Courtney Allen, Melissa S. Bennett

Cartoons: Rich Tennant, www.the5thwave.com

Production

Project Coordinator: Nancee Reeves

Layout and Graphics: Stephanie Jumper, Michael Kruzil, Heather Ryan, Jacque Schneider, Julie Trippetti,

Proofreaders: Angel Perez, Brian H. Walls

Indexer: Joan Griffitts

Publishing and Editorial for Consumer Dummies

Diane Graves Steele, Vice President and Publisher, Consumer Dummies

Joyce Pepple, Acquisitions Director, Consumer Dummies

Kristin A. Cocks, Product Development Director, Consumer Dummies

Michael Spring, Vice President and Publisher, Travel

Brice Gosnell, Associate Publisher, Travel

Kelly Regan, Editorial Director, Travel

Publishing for Technology Dummies

Andy Cummings, Vice President and Publisher, Dummies Technology/General User

Composition Services

Gerry Fahey, Vice President of Production Services

Debbie Stailey, Director of Composition Services

Table of Contents

The 5th Wave

By Rich Tennant

"I know it's a popular American expression, but you just don't say 'Hasta la vista, baby'—to a nun."

Introduction

• •

As society becomes more international in nature, knowing how to say at least a few words in other languages becomes increasingly useful. Inexpensive airfares make travel abroad a more realistic option. Global business environments necessitate overseas travel. You just may have friends and neighbors who speak other languages, or you may want to get in touch with your heritage by learning a little bit of the language that your ancestors spoke.

Whatever your reason for wanting to acquire some Spanish, this book can help. We're not promising fluency here, but if you want to greet someone, purchase a ticket, or order off a menu in Spanish, you need look no further than *Spanish Phrases For Dummies.*

About This Book

This book isn't like a class that you have to drag yourself to twice a week for a specified period of time. You can use this book however you want to, whether your goal is to know some words and phrases to help you get around when you visit the countries of Central or South America, travel to Spain, or you simply want to be able to say, "Hello, how are you?" to your Spanish-speaking neighbor. Go through this book at your own pace, reading as much or as little at a time as you like. You don't have to trudge through the chapters in order, either; just read the sections that interest you.

If you've never taken Spanish lessons before, you may want to read Chapters 1 and 2 before tackling the later ones. These chapters give you some of the basics that you need to know about the language, such as how to pronounce the various sounds.

Conventions Used in This Book

To make this book easy for you to navigate, we've set up a couple of conventions:

- ✔ Spanish terms are set in **boldface** to make them stand out.

- ✔ Pronunciations, set in *italics*, follow the Spanish terms.

   Stressed syllables are <u>underlined</u> in the pronunciation.

- ✔ Memorizing key words and phrases is important in language learning, so we collect the important words in a chapter or section into a list with the heading "Words to Know." Spanish nouns have genders, which determines which article each noun takes. In the Words to Know lists, we include the article for each noun so that you memorize it at the same time as the noun.

Also note that because each language has its own ways of expressing ideas, the English translations that we provide for the Spanish terms may not be exactly literal. We want you to know the gist of what someone is saying, not just the words that are being said. For example, you can translate the Spanish phrase **de nada** *(deh <u>nah</u>-dah)* literally as "of nothing," but the phrase really means "you're welcome." This book gives the "you're welcome" translation.

Foolish Assumptions

To write this book, we had to make some assumptions about who you are and what you want. Here are the assumptions that we've made about you:

- ✔ You know no Spanish — or if you took Spanish back in school, you don't remember a word of it.

- ✔ You're not looking for a book that will make you fluent in Spanish; you just want to know some words, phrases, and sentence constructions so you can communicate basic information in Spanish.

- ✔ You don't want to have to memorize long lists of vocabulary words or a bunch of boring grammar rules.

- ✔ You want to have fun and learn a little bit of Spanish at the same time.

If these statements apply to you, you've found the right book!

Icons Used in This Book

You may be looking for particular information while reading this book. To make certain types of information easier for you to find, we've placed the following icons in the left-hand margins throughout the book:

This icon highlights tips that can make learning Spanish easier.

To ensure that you don't forget important stuff, this icon serves as a reminder, like a string tied around your finger.

Languages are full of quirks that may trip you up if you're not prepared for them. This icon points to discussions of these weird grammar rules.

If you're looking for information about Spanish-speaking culture and travel, look for these icons. They draw your attention to interesting tidbits about the countries in which Spanish is spoken.

Where to Go from Here

Learning a language is all about jumping in and giving it a try (no matter how bad your pronunciation is at first). So make the leap! Start at the beginning or pick a chapter that interests you. Just make sure that you have fun!

Chapter 1

I Say It How?
Speaking Spanish

. . . .

In This Chapter

▶ Recognizing the Spanish you already know

▶ Saying it right (basic pronunciation)

▶ Diving into some typical expressions

. . . .

*I*f you're familiar with the term "Latin Lover," you may not be surprised to know that Spanish is called a Romance language. But the romance we're talking about here isn't exactly the Latin Lover type — unless you love to learn Latin.

Spanish (as well as several other languages, such as Italian, French, Romanian, and Portuguese) is a Romance language because its origins are in the Latin of ancient Rome. Because of that common origin, Romance languages have many similarities in grammar and the way they sound. (The fact that they all sound so romantic when spoken is purely a bonus!) For example, **casa** *(kah-sah),* the word for "house," is identical in looks, meaning, and sound whether you speak Portuguese, Italian, or Spanish.

This book concentrates on the Spanish spoken in Latin America. Throughout the book, we also explore the differences in the words used in these 19 countries and mention some variations in pronunciation. Latin America consists of all of the Western Hemisphere with the exception of Canada, the United States, the British and French-speaking Guyanas; and a few islands in the Caribbean, such as Jamaica, Haiti, and Curaçao, where locals speak English, French, or Dutch.

You Already Know Some Spanish

The English language is like an ever-growing entity that, with great wisdom, absorbs what it needs from other cultures and languages. You can find many correspondences between English and Spanish in the words that come from both Latin and French roots. These words can cause both delight and embarrassment. The delight comes in the words where the similar sounds also give similar meanings. The embarrassment comes from words where the sounds and even the roots are the same, but the meanings are completely different.

Among the delightful discoveries among similarities between the languages are words like **soprano** *(soh-prah-noh)* (soprano), **pronto** *(prohn-toh)* (right away, soon), and thousands of others that differ by just one or two letters, such as **conclusión** *(kohn-kloo-see ohn)* (conclusion), **composición** *(kohm-poh-see-see-ohn)* (composition), **libertad** *(lee-bvehr-tahd)* (liberty), **economía** *(eh-koh-noh-meeah)* (economy), **invención** *(een-bvehn-see-ohn)* (invention), and **presidente** *(preh-see-dehn-teh)* (president).

Beware of false friends

The trouble begins in the world of words that French linguists have designated as false friends. You can't trust fool's gold, false friends, or all word similarities. Within the groups of false friends, you may find words that look very similar to English words and even have the same roots, yet they mean completely different things. One that comes to mind is the word "actual," which has very different meanings in English and Spanish. In English, you know that it means "real, in reality, or the very one." Not so in Spanish. **Actual** (*ahk-too*<u>*ahl*</u>) in Spanish means "present; current; belonging to this moment, this day, or this year."

Another example is the adjective "embarrassed," that in English means ashamed or encumbered. In Spanish, **embarazada** (*ehm-bvah-rah-<u>sah</u>-dah*) is the adjective that comes from the same root as the English word, yet it's use nowadays almost exclusively means "pregnant." So you can say in English that you're a little embarrassed, but in Spanish you can't be just a little embarazada. Either you're pregnant or you're not.

Some crossover influence

Word trouble ends at the point where a word originating in English is absorbed into Spanish or vice versa. The proximity of the United States to Mexico produces a change in the Spanish spoken south of the U.S. border. An example is the word "car." In Mexico, people say **carro** (<u>*kah*</u>-*rroh*). In South America, on the other hand, people say **auto** (<u>*ahoo*</u>-*toh*). In Spain, people say **coche** (<u>*koh*</u>-*cheh*).

Here are just a few examples of Spanish words that you already know because English uses them, too:

- ✔ You've been to a **rodeo** (*roh*-<u>*deh*</u>-*oh*) or a **fiesta** (*fee*<u>*ehs*</u>-*tah*).

- ✔ You may have taken a **siesta** (*see*<u>*ehs*</u>-*tah*) or two.

- ✔ You probably know at least one **señorita** (*seh-nyoh*-<u>*ree*</u>-*tah*), and you surely have an **amigo** (*ah-*<u>*mee*</u>-*goh*). Maybe you'll even see him **mañana** (*mah-*<u>*nyah*</u>-*nah*).

- ✔ You already know the names of places like **Los Angeles** (*lohs* <u>*ahn*</u>-*Heh-lehs*) (the angels), **San Francisco** (*sahn frahn-*<u>*sees*</u>-*koh*) (St. Francis), **La Jolla** (*la* <u>*Hoh*</u>-*yah*) (the jewel), **Florida** (*floh-*<u>*ree*</u>-*dah*) (the blooming one), and **Puerto Rico** (<u>*pooehr*</u>-*toh* <u>*ree*</u>-*koh*) (rich harbor).

- ✔ You've eaten a **tortilla** *(tohr-<u>tee</u>-lyah)*, a **taco** *(<u>tah</u>-koh)*, or a **burrito** *(bvoo-<u>rree</u>-toh)*.

- ✔ You fancy the **tango** *(<u>tahn</u>-goh)*, the **bolero** *(bvo-<u>leh</u>-roh)*, or the **rumba** *(<u>room</u>-bvah)*. Or you may dance the **cumbia** *(<u>koom</u>-bveeah)*.

- ✔ You have a friend named **Juanita** *(Hooah-<u>nee</u>-tah)*, **Anita** *(ah-<u>nee</u>-tah)*, or **Clara** *(<u>klah</u>-rah)*.

Reciting Your ABC's

Correct pronunciation is key to avoiding misunder-standings. The following sections present some basic guidelines for proper pronunciation.

Throughout this book, you can find the pro-nunciation of a Spanish word next to it in parentheses, which we call *pronunciation brackets*. Within the pronunciation brackets, we separate all the words that have more than one syllable with a hyphen, like this: *(<u>kah</u>-sah)*. An underlined syllable within the pronunciation brackets tells you to accent, or stress, that syllable. We say much more about stress in the section "Pronunciation and Stress" later in this chapter. But don't let yourself get stressed out (pardon the pun). We explain each part of the language sepa-rately, and the pieces quickly fall into place. Promise!

In the following sections, we comment on some let-ters of the alphabet from the Spanish point of view to help you to understand Spanish pronunciations. Here is the basic Spanish alphabet and its pronunciation:

a *(ah)*   **e** *(eh)*

b *(bveh)*   **f** *(<u>eh</u>-feh)*

c *(seh)*   **g** *(Heh)*

d *(deh)*   **h** *(<u>ah</u>-cheh)*

i *(ee)*

j *(Hoh-tah)*

k *(kah)*

l *(eh-leh)*

m *(eh-meh)*

n *(eh-neh)*

ñ *(eh-nyeh)*

o *(oh)*

p *(peh)*

q *(koo)*

r *(eh-reh)*

s *(eh-seh)*

t *(teh)*

u *(oo)*

v *(bveh)*

w *(doh-bleh bveh)*
(oo – bveh doh-bvleh)
(Spain)

x *(eh-kees)*

y *(ee gree eh-gah)*

z *(seh-tah)*

Spanish also includes some double letters in its alphabet: **ch** *(cheh),* **ll** *(ye),* and **rr** *(a trilled r).*

We don't go through every letter of the alphabet in the sections that follow, only those that you use differently in Spanish than in English. The differences can lie in pronunciation, the way they look, in the fact that you seldom see the letters, or that you don't pronounce them at all.

Consonants

Consonants tend to sound the same in English and Spanish. We explain the few differences that you can find.

Inside the Spanish-speaking world itself, you find that you may pronounce consonants differently than in English. For example, in Spain, the consonant *z* is pronounced like the *th* in the English word *thesis.* (Latin Americans don't use this sound; in all 19 Spanish-speaking countries in the Western hemisphere, *z* and *s* sound the same.)

In the Spanish speaker's mind, a consonant
is any sound that needs to have a vowel next
to it when you pronounce it. For example,
saying the letter *t* by itself may be difficult
for a Spanish speaker. To the Spanish ear,
pronouncing *t* sounds like **te** *(teh)*. Likewise,
the Spanish speaker says **ese** *(eh-seh)* when
pronouncing the letter *s*.

Only a few consonants in Spanish differ from their
English counterparts. The following sections look
more closely at the behavior and pronunciation of
these consonants.

The letter K

In Spanish, the letter *k* is used only in words that have
their origin in foreign languages. More often than not,
this letter is seen in **kilo** *(kee-loh)*, meaning thousand
in Greek. An example is **kilómetro** *(kee-loh-meh-troh)*
(kilometer) — a thousand-meter measure for distance.

The letter H

In Spanish, the letter *h* is always mute. That's it!

The pronunciation brackets throughout this book
often include the letter *h*. These *h*'s generally signal
certain vowel sounds, which we cover in the section
"Vowels" later in this chapter. In the pronunciation
brackets, the Spanish *h* simply doesn't appear
because it's mute.

Following are some examples of the Spanish *h*:

✔ **Huayapan** *(ooah-yah-pahn)* (name of a village in
  Mexico)

✔ **hueso** *(ooeh-soh)* (bone)

✔ **huevo** *(ooeh-bvoh)* (egg)

The letter J

The consonant *j* sounds like a guttural *h*. Normally,
you say *h* quite softly, as though you're just breathing
out. Now, say your *h*, but gently raise the back of your

tongue, as if you were saying *k*. Push the air out really hard, and you get the sound. Try it! It sounds like you're gargling, doesn't it?

To signal that you need to make this sound, we use a capital letter *H* within the pronunciation brackets.

Now try the sound out on these words:

- ✔ **Cajamarca** *(kah-Hah-mahr-kah)* (the name of a city in Peru)
- ✔ **cajeta** *(kah-Heh-tah)* (a delicious, thick sauce made of milk and sugar)
- ✔ **cajón** *(kah-Hohn)* (big box)
- ✔ **jadeo** *(Hah-deh-oh)* (panting)
- ✔ **Jijón** *(Hee-Hohn)* (the name of a city in Spain)
- ✔ **jota** *(Hoh-tah)* (the Spanish name for the letter *j*; also the name of a folk dance in Spain.)
- ✔ **tijera** *(tee-Heh-rah)* (scissors)

The letter C

The letter *c*, in front of the vowels *a, o,* and *u,* sounds like the English *k*. We use the letter *k* in the pronunciation brackets to signal this sound. The following list gives you some examples:

- ✔ **acabar** *(ah-kah-bvahr)* (to finish)
- ✔ **café** *(kah-feh)* (coffee)
- ✔ **casa** *(kah-sah)* (house)
- ✔ **ocaso** *(oh-kah-soh)* (sunset)

When the letter *c* is in front of the vowels *e* and *i,* it sounds like the English *s*. In the pronunciation brackets, we signal this sound as *s*. The following list has some examples:

- ✔ **acero** *(ah-seh-roh)* (steel)
- ✔ **cero** *(seh-roh)* (zero)
- ✔ **cine** *(see-neh)* (cinema)

In much of Spain — primarily the north and central parts — the letter *c* is pronounced like the *th* in thanks when placed before the vowels *e* and *i*.

The letters S and Z

In Latin American Spanish, the letters *s* and *z* always sound like the English letter *s*. We use the letter *s* in the pronunciation brackets to signal this sound. The following list gives you some examples:

- ✔ **asiento** (*ah-see<u>ehn</u>-toh*) (seat)

- ✔ **sol** (*sohl*) (sun)

- ✔ **zarzuela** (*sahr-soo<u>eh</u>-lah*) (Spanish-style operetta)

In Spain, *z* also has the sound of the *th* in thanks, rather than the *s* sound prevalent in Latin America.

The letters B and V

The letters *b* and *v* are pronounced the same, the sound being somewhere in-between the two letters. This in-between is a fuzzy, bland sound — closer to *v* than to *b*. If you position your lips and teeth to make a *v* sound, and then try to make a *b* sound, you have it. To remind you to make this sound, we use *bv* in our pronunciation brackets, for both *b* and *v*. Here are some examples:

- ✔ **cabeza** (*kah-<u>bveh</u>-sah*) (head)

- ✔ **vida** (*<u>bvee</u>-dah*) (life)

- ✔ **violín** (*bveeoh-<u>leen</u>*) (violin)

The letter Q

Spanish doesn't use the letter *k* very much; when the language wants a *k* sound in front of the vowels *e* and *i,* it unfolds the letter combination *qu*. So when you see the word **queso** (*<u>keh</u>-soh*) (cheese), you immediately know that you say the _k_ sound. Here are some examples of the Spanish letter _q_, which we indicate by the letter _k_ in pronunciation brackets:

- **Coquimbo** _(koh-<u>keem</u>-bvoh)_ (the name of a city in Chile)
- **paquete** _(pah-<u>keh</u>-teh)_ (package)
- **pequeño** _(peh-<u>keh</u>-nyoh)_ (small)
- **tequila** _(teh-<u>kee</u>-lah)_ (Mexican liquor, spirits)

The letter G

In Spanish the letter _g_ has a double personality, like the letter _c_. When you combine the letter _g_ with a consonant or when you see it in front of the vowels _a, o,_ and _u,_ it sounds like the _g_ in goose. Here are some examples:

- **begonia** _(bveh-<u>goh</u>-neeah)_ (begonia)
- **gato** _(<u>gah</u>-toh)_ (cat)
- **gracias** _(<u>grah</u>-seeahs)_ (thank you)
- **pagado** _(pah-<u>gah</u>-doh)_ (paid for)

The _g_ changes personality in front of the vowels _e_ and _i._ It sounds like the Spanish _j,_ which we signal with the capital _H_ in our pronunciation brackets:

- **agenda** _(ah-<u>Hehn</u>-dah)_ (agenda; date book)
- **gerente** _(Heh-<u>rehn</u>-teh)_ (manager)

To hear the sound _g_ (as in goat) in front of the vowels _e_ and _i,_ you must insert a _u,_ making **gue** and **gui.** To remind you to make the goat sound (no, no, not mme-hehe, but _g_) we use _gh_ in our pronunciation brackets. Some examples:

- **guía** _(gheeah)_ (guide)
- **guiño** _(<u>ghee</u>-nyoh)_ (wink)
- **guerra** _(<u>gheh</u>-rrah)_ (war)

Double consonants

Spanish has two double consonants: **ll** and **rr.** They're considered a singular letter, and each has a singular sound. Because these consonants are considered singular, they stick together when you separate syllables. For example, the word **calle** *(kah-yeh)* (street) appears as **ca-lle.** And **torre** *(toh-rreh)* (tower) separates into **to-rre.**

The letter LL

The **ll** consonant sounds like the *y* in the English word yes, except in Argentina and Uruguay.

Argentineans and Uruguayans pronounce this consonant as the sound that happens when you have your lips pursed to say *s* and then make the *z* sound through them. Try it. Fun, isn't it? But really, the sound isn't that difficult to make because you can find the English equivalent in words like measure and pleasure. The way you say those *s* sounds is exactly how **ll** is pronounced in Argentina and Uruguay.

Throughout this book, we use the sound like the English *y* in the word yes, which is how **ll** is pronounced in 18 of the 20 Spanish-speaking countries of Latin America. In the pronunciation brackets, we use *y* to signal this sound.

Now try the **ll** sound, using the *y* sound, in the following examples:

- ✔ **brillo** *(bvree-yoh)* (shine)
- ✔ **llama** *(yah-mah)* (flame; also the name of an animal in Peru)
- ✔ **lluvia** *(yoo-bveeah)* (rain)

The letter RR

The **rr** sounds like a strongly rolled *r.* In fact, every *r* is strongly rolled in Spanish, but the double one is the real winner. To roll an *r,* curl your tongue against the roof of your mouth as you finish the *r* sound. It should trill.

An easy way to make this sound is to say the letter *r* as though you're pretending to sound like an outboard motor. Spanish speakers take special pleasure in rolling their **rr**'s. One fun thing about **rr** is that no words begin with it. Isn't that a relief! In pronunciation brackets, we simply signal this sound as **rr**.

Play with these words:

- ✔ **carrera** *(kah-rreh-rah)* (race; profession)
- ✔ **correo** *(koh-rreh-oh)* (mail, post)
- ✔ **tierra** *(teeeh-rrah)* (land)

The letter Y

This letter represents sounds that are very similar to those of **ll**. The people of both Argentina and Uruguay pronounce this sound differently from the rest of Latin America. We advise that you pronounce it as the English *y* in yes. In the pronunciation brackets, we signal this sound as **y**. The following list gives you some examples:

- ✔ **playa** *(plah-yah)* (beach)
- ✔ **yema** *(yeh-mah)* (yolk; also finger tip)
- ✔ **yodo** *(yoh-doh)* (Iodine)

In Spanish, the letter *y* is never a vowel, always a consonant.

The letter Ñ

When you see a wiggly line on top of the letter *n* that looks like **ñ**, use the *ny* sound that you use for the English word canyon. The wiggly line is called a **tilde** *(teel-deh)*. In pronunciation brackets, we show this sound as *ny*. The following list has some examples:

- ✔ **cuñado** *(koo-nyah-doh)* (brother-in-law)
- ✔ **mañana** *(mah-nyah-nah)* (tomorrow)
- ✔ **niña** *(nee-nyah)* (girl)

Vowels

If you want your Spanish to sound like a native's, you have to concentrate on your vowels.

The biggest difference between English and Spanish is almost certainly in the way speakers write and pronounce the vowels. By now, you may be well aware that one vowel in English can have more than one sound. Look, for instance, at *fat* and *fate*. Both words have the vowel *a,* but they're pronounced much differently from each other. The good news is that in Spanish, you always say the vowels one way, and one way only.

The upcoming sections discuss the five vowels — which are the only vowel sounds in Spanish. They're **a** *(ah),* **e** *(eh),* **i** *(ee),* **o** *(oh),* **u** *(oo).* Spanish sees each of these vowels by itself and makes other sounds by combining the vowels in twos.

The vowel A

As children, almost everybody sings their ABC's. In Spanish, the English *a* that starts off the song, is pronounced *ah.* The easiest way to remember how to pronounce the letter *a* in Spanish is to sing the chorus of the Christmas carol "Deck the Halls" to yourself. Do you remember the chorus? "Fa la la la la, la la, la la." We write this sound as *ah* in the pronunciation brackets.

The following list gives you some sample words to practice. Remember that you pronounce each and every *a* exactly the same way:

- ✔ **Caracas** *(kah-rah-kas)* (a city in Venezuela)
- ✔ **mapa** *(mah-pah)* (map)
- ✔ **Guadalajara** *(gooah-dah-lah-Hah-rah)* (a city in Mexico)

The vowel E

To get an idea of how the Spanish *e* sounds, smile gently, open your mouth a bit and say "eh." The sound should be like the *e* in the English word pen. In our pronunciation brackets, this vowel appears as *eh*.

Try these *e* words:

- ✔ **pelele** *(peh-leh-leh)* (rag doll; puppet)
- ✔ **pelo** *(peh-loh)* (hair)
- ✔ **seco** *(seh-koh)* (dry)

The vowel I

In Spanish, the vowel *i* sounds like the *ee* in seen, but just a touch shorter. To give you an example, when English speakers say *feet* or *street,* the Spanish speaker hears what sounds almost like two *i*'s.

We signal this sound as *ee* in our pronunciation brackets. The following list has some examples:

- ✔ **irritar** *(ee-rree-tahr)* (to irritate)
- ✔ **piña** *(pee-nyah)* (pineapple)
- ✔ **pintar** *(peen-tahr)* (to paint)

The vowel O

The Spanish put their mouths in a rounded position, as if to breathe a kiss over a flower, and keeping it in that position, say *o.* It sounds like the *o* in floor, but a bit shorter. We signal this sound as *oh* in the pronunciation brackets.

Try practicing the sound on these words:

- ✔ **coco** *(koh-koh)* (coconut)
- ✔ **Orinoco** *(oh-ree-noh-koh)* (a river in Venezuela)
- ✔ **Oruro** *(oh-roo-roh)* (a city in Bolivia)
- ✔ **toronja** *(toh-rohn-Hah)* (grapefruit)

The vowel U

The fifth and last vowel in Spanish is the *u,* and it sounds like the *oo* in moon or raccoon, but just a

touch shorter. We write this sound as *oo* in the pronunciation brackets. Here are some examples of the *u*
sound:

- ✔ **cuna** (*<u>koo</u>-nah*) (cradle)
- ✔ **cuñado** (*koo-<u>nyah</u>-doh*) (brother-in-law)
- ✔ **cúrcuma** (*<u>koor</u>-koo-mah*) (turmeric)
- ✔ **curioso** (*koo-ree<u>oh</u>-soh*) (curious)
- ✔ **fruta** (*<u>froo</u>-tah*) (fruit)
- ✔ **luna** (*<u>loo</u>-nah*) (moon)
- ✔ **tuna** (*<u>too</u>-nah*) (prickle pear)

The diphthongs

Diphthong comes from Greek, where *di* means two,
and *thong* comes from a very similar word meaning
sound or voice. Very simply, it means double sound.
There. That's easier.

The Spanish word is **diptongo** (*deep-<u>tohn</u>-goh*).
Diptongos are the combination of two vowels, from the
Spanish-speaking point of view. For instance, *i* and *o*
combine to make *io* as in **patio** (*<u>pah</u>-teeoh*) (courtyard
or patio).

Joining the weak to the strong

Diptongos are always made up of a weak and
a strong vowel. Calling vowels "weak" or
"strong" is a convention of the Spanish language. The convention comes from the fact
that the so-called strong vowel is always
dominant in the diphthong. To the Spanish
speaker, *i* and *u* are weak vowels, leaving *a, e,*
and *o* as strong ones.

To visualize this weak or strong concept,
consider a piccolo flute and a bass horn. The
sound of the piccolo is definitely more like the
Spanish *i* and *u,* while the base horn sounds
more like the Spanish *a, e,* and especially *o.*

Any combination of one strong and one weak vowel is a **diptongo** *(deep-tohn-goh),* which means that they belong together in the same syllable. In fact, they're not only together, they're stuck like superglue; you can't separate them.

In the **diptongo,** the stress falls on the strong vowel (more about stress in the section "Pronunciation and Stress" later in this chapter). An accent mark alerts you when the stress falls on the weak vowel. (More about accents in the section "Looking for accented vowels" later in this chapter, too.) In the combination of two weak vowels, the stress is on the second one.

Try these examples of diphthongs:

- ✔ **bueno** *(bvooeh-noh)* (good)
- ✔ **cuando** *(kooahn-doh)* (when)
- ✔ **fiar** *(feeahr)* (sell on credit)
- ✔ **fuera** *(fooeh-rah)* (outside)
- ✔ **suizo** *(sooee-soh)* (Swiss)
- ✔ **viudo** *(bveeoo-doh)* (widower)

Separating the strong from the strong

When you combine two strong vowels, they don't form a diphthong. Instead, the vowels retain their separate values, so you must put them into separate syllables. Here are some examples:

- ✔ **aorta** *(ah-ohr-tah)* (aorta) (See! Just like in English!)
- ✔ **feo** *(feh-oh)* (ugly)
- ✔ **marea** *(mah-reh-ah)* (tide)
- ✔ **mareo** *(mah-reh-oh)* (dizziness)

Pronunciation and Stress

In Spanish, you stress one syllable in every word. Stress is the accent that you put on a syllable as you speak it. One syllable always gets more stress than the others. In single-syllable words, finding the stress is easy. But many words have more than one syllable, and that's when the situation becomes stressful.

Looking for stress, normally

Can you believe that you're looking for stress? In Spanish, the right stress at the right time is a good thing, and fortunately, stress in Spanish is easy to control. If you have no written accent, you have two possibilities:

- ✔ The word is stressed next to the last syllable if it ends in a vowel, an *n,* or an *s.* Here are some examples:

  camas *(<u>kah</u>-mahs)* (beds)

  mariposas *(mah-ree-<u>poh</u>-sahs)* (butterflies)

  pollo *(<u>poh</u>-yoh)* (chicken)

- ✔ The word is stressed on the last syllable when it ends in a consonant that isn't an *n* or *s.* Look at these examples:

  cantar *(kahn-<u>tahr</u>)* (to sing)

  feliz *(feh-<u>lees</u>)* (happy)

If a word isn't stressed in either of these two ways, the word will have an accent mark on it to indicate where you should place the stress.

Looking for accented vowels

One good thing about having the accent mark on a vowel is that you can tell immediately where the stress is just by looking at the word.

The accent mark doesn't affect how you pronounce the vowel, just which syllable you stress.

Here are some examples of words with accent marks on a vowel:

- **balcón** *(bahl-kohn)* (balcony)
- **carácter** *(kah-rahk-tehr)* (character, personality)
- **fotógrafo** *(foh-toh-grah-foh)* (photographer)
- **pájaro** *(pah-Hah-roh)* (bird)

Understanding accents on diphthongs

An accent in a diphthong shows you which vowel to stress. Take a look at these examples:

- **¡Adiós!** *(ah-deeohs)* (Good bye!)
- **¡Buenos días!** *(bvooeh-nohs deeahs)* (Good morning!)
- **¿Decía?** *(deh-seeah)* (You were saying?)
- **tía** *(teeah)* (aunt)

¡Punctuation Plus!

Did you notice the unfamiliar punctuation in **¡Buenos días!**, **¿Decía?**, and **¡Adiós!**? Spanish indicates the mood (or tone) of what you're saying both at the beginning and at the end of a question or exclamation phrase, as in **¿Decía?** *(deh-seeah)* (You were saying?) or **¡Decía!** *(dehsee-ah)* (You were saying!).

This punctuation is the verbal equivalent of making gestures, which you can see in the following examples:

- **¿Dónde está?** *(dohn-deh ehs-tah)* (Where is it?)
- **¡Qué maravilla!** *(keh mah-rah-bvee-yah)* (How wonderful!)

Some Basic Phrases to Know

The following phrases can get you through a number of awkward pauses as you think of the right word:

✔ **¡Olé!** *(oh- leh)* (Great!; Superb!; Keep going!)

This very Spanish expression is used during bullfights in Mexico and Peru.

✔ **¿Quiubo?** *(kee oo-boh)* (Hello, what's happening?)

✔ **¿De veras?** *(deh bveh-rahs)* (Really?)

This phrase signals slight disbelief.

✔ **¡No me digas!** *(noh meh dee-gahs)* (You don't say!)

This phrase also shows disbelief.

Chapter 2

Grammar on a Diet: Just the Basics

* *

In This Chapter

▶ Understanding simple sentence construction

▶ Forming questions

▶ Addressing that whole gender

▶ Looking at the formal and informal you

* *

To be honest, studying grammar isn't the most enjoyable part of discovering a language. Just keep in mind that what you get from the nitty-gritty of this grammar chapter can help you in other places, too. And remember that you don't need to chew your way through this chapter in one single meal. When we want to draw your attention to something in this chapter when you're elsewhere in the book, we tell you.

Then again, you may be the kind of person who truly enjoys grammar and structure. If so, you're in for a treat!

Sentence Construction

In Spanish, as in English, you form a sentence by combining a subject, a verb, and perhaps further descriptive information. For example:

La casa es grande. (lah _kah_-sah ehs _grahn_-deh) (The house is big.)

Here, the subject of the sentence is **la casa** *(lah kah-sah)* (the house); then comes the verb, **es** *(ehs)* (is); after that comes the adjective, **grande** *(grahn-deh)* (big), which describes the house. In Spanish, the three basic parts of a sentence go in this order.

Here are some more examples:

✔ **La mujer es bella.** *(lah moo-Hehr ehs bveh-yah)* (The woman is beautiful.)

✔ **El hombre es buen mozo.** *(ehl ohm-bvreh ehs bvooehn moh-soh)* (The man is handsome.)

✔ **Las calles son largas.** *(lahs kah-yehs sohn lahr-gahs)* (The streets are long.)

Verbs

Spanish verbs all end with one of three letter combinations: **-ar, -er,** or **-ir.** You find both regular and irregular verbs with all three endings. As you may guess, regular verbs all form different tenses (past, present, and future) and persons (I/we, you, and he/she/it/they) in the same way — a process called *conjugation.* So, if you know how to conjugate one regular verb, you can determine the conjugation of all regular verbs like it.

The form of irregular verbs, however, can change when you least expect it. Ultimately, you need to memorize the conjugation of each irregular verb to ensure that you use it correctly. (Don't worry if you make a mistake; most Spanish speakers can figure out what you want to say, even if your verb ending isn't quite right.)

Regular verbs

In all regular verbs in Spanish, the first section of the word — its *root* — stays constant. For example, the verb **trabajar** *(trah-bvah-Hahr)* (to work) is a regular verb ending in **-ar.** The root **trabaj-** stays the same throughout conjugation. Table 2-1 shows you how you conjugate this verb — and all other regular verbs ending with **-ar.**

Table 2-1   Three Tenses of Trabajar (to Work)

Conjugation	Pronunciation
Present tense:	
yo trabajo	*yoh trah-bvah-Hoh*
tú trabajas	*too trah-bvah-Hahs*
él, ella, ello, uno, usted trabaja	*ehl, eh-yah, eh-yoh, oo-noh, oos-tehd trah-bvah-Hah*
nosotros trabajamos	*noh-soh-trohs trah-bvah-Hah-mohs*
vosotros trabajáis	*bvoh-soh-trohs trah-bvah-Hahees*
ellos, ellas, ustedes trabajan	*eh-yohs, eh-yahs, oos-teh-dehs trah-bvah-Hahn*
Past tense:	
yo trabajé	*yoh trah-bvah-Heh*
tú trabajaste	*too trah-bvah-Hahs-teh*
él, ella, ello, uno, usted trabajó	*ehl, eh-yah, eh-yoh, oo-noh, oos-tehd trah- bvah-Hoh*
nosotros trabajamos	*noh-soh-trohs trah-bvah-Hah-mohs*
vosotros trabajásteis	*bvoh-soh-trohs trah-bvah-Hahs-tehees*
ellos, ellas, ustedes trabajaron	*eh-yohs, eh-yahs, oos-teh-dehs trah-bvah-Hah-ron*

(continued)

Table 2-1 *(continued)*

Conjugation	Pronunciation
Future tense:	
yo trabajaré	*yoh trah-bvah-Hah-reh*
tú trabajarás	*too trah-bvah-Hah-rahs*
él, ella, ello, uno, usted trabajará	*ehl, eh-yah, eh-yoh, oo-noh, oos-tehd trah-bvah-Hah-rah*
nosotros trabajaremos	*noh-soh-trohs trah-bvah-Hah-reh-mohs*
vosotros trabajaréis	*bvoh-soh-trohs trah-bvah-Hah-rehees*
ellos, ellas, ustedes trabajarán	*eh-yohs, eh-yahs, oos-teh-dehs trah-bvah-Hah-ran*

Irregular verbs

In irregular verbs, the root, and at times the endings of the verb, keep changing, which complicates matters.

An example is the verb **tener** *(teh-nehr)* (to have). As Table 2-2 shows, the root of the verb, **ten-**, changes into **teng-** and **tien-**. But look carefully at the endings, and you can see that some things remain the same.

Table 2-2   Three Tenses of Tener (to Have)

Conjugation	Pronunciation
Present tense:	
yo tengo	yoh tehn-goh
tú tienes	too tee-eh-nehs

Conjugation	Pronunciation
él, ella, ello, uno, usted tiene	ehl, <u>eh</u>-yah, <u>eh</u>-yoh, <u>oo</u>-noh, oos-<u>tehd</u> tee-<u>eh</u>-neh
nosotros tenemos	noh-<u>soh</u>-trohs teh-<u>neh</u>-mohs
vosotros tenéis	bvoh-<u>soh</u>-trohs teh-<u>neh</u>ees
ellos, ellas, ustedes tienen	<u>eh</u>-yohs, <u>eh</u>-yahs, oos-<u>teh</u>-dehs tee-<u>eh</u>-nehn
Past tense:	
yo tuve	yoh <u>too</u>-bveh
tú tuviste	too too-<u>bvees</u>-teh
él, ella, ello, uno, usted tuvo	ehl, <u>eh</u>-yah, <u>eh</u>-yoh, <u>oo</u>-noh, oos-<u>tehd</u> <u>too</u>-bvoh
nosotros tuvimos	noh-<u>soh</u>-trohs too-<u>bvee</u>-mohs
vosotros tuvisteis	bvoh-<u>soh</u>-trohs too-<u>bvees</u>-tehees
ellos, ellas, ustedes tuvieron	<u>eh</u>-yohs, <u>eh</u>-yahs, oos-<u>teh</u>-dehs too-bvee-<u>eh</u>-rohn
Future tense:	
yo tendre	yoh tehn-<u>dreh</u>
tú tendrás	too tehn-<u>drahs</u>
él, ella, ello, uno, usted tendrá	ehl, <u>eh</u>-yah, <u>eh</u>-yoh, <u>oo</u>-noh, oos-<u>tehd</u> tehn-<u>drah</u>
nosotros tendremos	noh-<u>soh</u>-trohs tehn-<u>dreh</u>-mohs
vosotros tendréis	bvoh-<u>soh</u>-trohs tehn-<u>dreh</u>ees
ellos, ellas, ustedes tendrán	<u>eh</u>-yohs, <u>eh</u>-yahs, oos-<u>teh</u>-dehs tehn-<u>drahn</u>

Extra verbs charts

The tables in this section give you the conjugation for the three categories of regular verbs, and a few irregular verbs.

Table 2-3 conjugates **hablar** *(ah-bvlahr)* (to speak), a regular verb ending with **-ar.**

Table 2-3	Regular -ar: Hablar (to speak)		
	Present	*Simple Past*	*Future*
yo (I)	hablo (speak)	hablé (spoke)	hablaré (will speak)
tú (you, informal)	hablas	hablaste	hablarás
Ud. (you, formal)	habla	habló	hablará
él/ella (he/she)	habla	habló	hablará
nosotros (we)	hablamos	hablamos	hablaremos
Uds. (you, formal)	hablan	hablaron	hablarán
ellos/ellas (they)	hablan	hablaron	hablarán

Table 2-4 conjugates **comer** *(kohm-ehr)* (to eat), a regular verb ending with **-er.**

Table 2-4	Regular -er: Comer (to Eat)		
	Present	*Simple Past*	*Future*
yo (I)	como (eat)	comí (ate)	comeré (will eat)
tú (you, informal)	comes	comiste	comerás
Ud. (you, formal)	come	comió	comerá
él/ella (he/she)	come	comió	comerá
nosotros (we)	comemos	comimos	comeremos
Uds. (you, formal)	comen	comieron	comerán
ellos/ellas (they)	comen	comieron	comerán

Table 2-5 conjugates **vivir** *(bvee-bveer)* (to live), a regular verb ending with **-ir**.

Table 2-5	Regular -ir: Vivir (to Live)		
	Present	*Simple Past*	*Future*
yo (I)	vivo (live)	viví (lived)	viviré (will live)
tú (you, informal)	vives	viviste	vivirás
Ud. (you, formal)	vive	vivió	vivirá
él/ella (he/she)	vive	vivió	vivirá
nosotros (we)	vivimos	vivimos	viviremos
Uds. (you, formal)	viven	vivieron	vivirán
ellos/ellas (they)	viven	vivieron	vivirán

Table 2-6 conjugates the irregular verb **estar** *(ehs-tahr)* (to be; location, state of condition).

Table 2-6	Irregular Estar (to Be)		
	Present	*Simple Past*	*Future*
yo (I)	estoy (am)	estuve (was)	estaré (will be)
tú (you, informal)	estás	estuviste	estarás
Ud. (you, formal)	está	estuvo	estará
él/ella (he/she)	está	estuvo	estará
nosotros (we)	estamos	estuvimos	estaremos
Uds. (you, formal)	están	estuvieron	estarán
ellos/ellas (they)	están	estuvieron	estarán

Table 2-7 conjugates the irregular verb **ser** *(sehr)* (to be; permanent state of condition).

Table 2-7	Irregular Ser (to Be)		
	Present	*Simple Past*	*Future*
yo (I)	soy (am)	fui (was)	seré (will be)
tú (you, informal)	eres	fuiste	serás
Ud. (you, formal)	es	fue	sera
él/ella (he/she)	es	fue	sera
nosotros (we)	somos	fuimos	seremos
Uds. (you, formal)	son	fueron	serán
ellos/ellas (they)	son	fueron	serán

Table 2-8 conjugates the reflexive verb **lavarse** *(lah-vahrs)* (to wash oneself).

Table 2-8	Reflexive Lavarse (to Wash Oneself)		
	Present	*Simple Past*	*Future*
yo (I)	me lavo	me lavé	me lavaré
tú (you, informal)	te lavas	te lavaste	te lavarás
Ud. (you, formal)	se lava	se lavó	se lavará
él/ella (he/she)	se lava	se lavó	se lavará
nosotros (we)	nos lavamos	nos lavamos	nos lavaremos
Uds. (you, formal)	se lavan	se lavaron	se lavarán
ellos/ellas (they)	se lavan	se lavaron	se lavarán

Forming Questions

We have some good news for you: Forming a question in Spanish is easy. You just have to reverse the order of the verb and the subject. You say **Ésta es . . .** (*ehs-tah ehs*) (This is . . .) in a regular sentence, but for a question, you say **¿Es ésta . . .?** (*ehs ehs-tah*) (Is this . . . ?). This change works the same as it does in English, when you say "This is . . ." and "Is this . . .?"

Check out this example:

✔ **Ésta es la puerta.** (*ehs-tah ehs lah poo-ehr-tah*)
(This is the door.)

✔ **¿Es ésta la puerta?** (*ehs ehs-tah lah poo-ehr-tah*)
(Is this the door?)

Now, suppose you want to answer in the negative. All you have to do is insert the word **no** before the verb (almost the way you do in English, but easier). An example:

✔ **¿Es ése el carro?** (*ehs eh-seh ehl kah-rroh*)
(Is that the car?)

✔ **No, ése no es el carro.** (*noh eh-seh noh ehs ehl kah-rro*) (No, that's not the car.)

English often includes the verb "do" in questions, but Spanish makes things easier on you. In Spanish, the word "do" is understood as part of the verb:

✔ **¿Vas al cine?** (*bvahs ahl see-neh*) (Do you go to the movies?)

✔ **Sí, voy.** (*see bvohy*) (Yes, I [do] go.)

In English, "Yes, I do" can mean many things (going to the movies, using your computer, making a phone call, and so on). In Spanish, you have to get a bit more specific:

✔ **¿Va tu padre al cine?** (*bvah too pah-dreh ahl see-neh*) (Does your father go to the movies?)

✔ **No, no va.** (*noh noh bvah*) (No, he doesn't go.)

We used the following sentences as affirmative statements in the earlier section about "Sentence Construction," and now we're using them to demonstrate the questioning (*interrogative*) and denying (*negative*) moods:

✔ **¿Es bella la mujer?** *(ehs bveh-yah lah moo-Hehr)* (Is the woman beautiful?)

✔ **La mujer no es bella.** *(lah moo-Hehr noh ehs bveh-yah)* (The woman isn't beautiful.)

✔ **¿Es buen mozo el hombre?** *(ehs bvooehn moh-soh ehl ohm-bvreh)* (Is the man handsome?)

✔ **El hombre no es buen mozo.** *(ehl ohm-bvreh noh ehs bvooehn moh-soh)* (The man isn't handsome.)

✔ **¿Son largas las calles?** *(sohn lahr-gahs lahs kah-yehs)* (Are the streets long?)

✔ **Las calles no son largas.** *(lahs kah-yehs noh sohn lahr-gahs)* (The streets aren't long.)

Pronouns in Hiding

For the most part, the Spanish language stays quite regular and to the point, which makes it easy to learn and speak. However, Spanish often hides the pronouns he, she, and it. The easy part with Spanish is that you don't have to say the pronoun — you can make a good guess about the intended pronoun simply from the verb form.

In English, you always use the pronoun before the verb. Not so in Spanish. Because each pronoun has its own verb form, Spanish generally omits the pronoun. Therefore, you say **Voy al cine** for "I go to the movies." Here are some other examples:

✔ **Están de vacaciones.** *(ehs-tahn deh bvah-kah-seeoh-nehs)* (They're on vacation.)

✔ **No es el carro.** *(noh ehs ehl kah-rroh)* (It's not the car.)

✔ **¿Tienen vino?** *(teeeh-nehn bvec noh)* (Do they or you have wine?)

That Whole Gender Thing

What Spanish lacks in pronouns, it makes up for by being very specific in other parts of a sentence.

You see, in Spanish, not just people, but everything in creation has gender!

When you refer to people and animals, you can easily understand gender use in Spanish because gender is a part of their essence.

A noun's gender conditions everything around it, just as your own gender conditions your lifestyle. For example, in English, the word "piano" has no gender. But in Spanish, the word **piano** *(pee-ah-noh)* ends in an *o,* and can therefore be only male. Consequently, piano has a male definite article before it — **el piano** *(ehl pee-ah-noh)* (the piano) or the male indefinite article **un piano** *(oon pee-ah-noh)* (a piano).

In English, you use the articles *the* and *a* or *an* without knowing the subject's gender, or even caring whether a plural or singular word comes after it — very comfortable, but also very vague. With Spanish articles, you can point out when you're referring to one or several specific beings or things, and in the same breath, you can specify their gender.

In Spanish, your reward for this precision is variety. Spanish has a "more is better" kind of policy — you have four different ways to say the: "The" can precede "the girl," "the girls," "the boy," "the boys," or any other subject you want to stick in!

✔ **el** *(ehl)* (the, singular masculine)

✔ **la** *(lah)* (the, singular feminine)

✔ **los** *(lohs)* (the, plural masculine)

✔ **las** *(lahs)* (the, plural feminine)

Here are four ways to say *a* or *an:*

- ✔ **un** *(oon)* (the masculine *a* or *an*)
- ✔ **una** *(<u>oo</u>-nah)* (the feminine *a* or *an*)
- ✔ **unos** *(<u>oo</u>-nohs)* (the masculine plural)
- ✔ **unas** *(<u>oo</u>-nahs)* (the feminine plural)

So, how do you know when to use which article? It's easy. When the noun ends in *o,* it's male. If a word ends in *a,* it's female.

Some exceptions to this rule exist, but they're pretty easy to figure out because they follow another rule — the *ma, pa, ta* rule, which holds that words ending in *ma, pa,* and *ta* are probably masculine, even though *a* is the last letter.

The easy part to remember is that when you see an *s* at the end of the word, you know the word is plural. Here are some examples:

- ✔ **el niño** *(ehl <u>nee</u>-nyoh)* (the boy)
- ✔ **los niños** *(lohs <u>nee</u>-nyohs)* (the boys [or the children])
- ✔ **un niño** *(oon <u>nee</u>-nyoh)* (a boy)
- ✔ **unos niños** *(<u>oo</u>-nohs <u>nee</u>-nyohs)* (some boys [or children])
- ✔ **la niña** *(lah <u>nee</u>-nyah)* (the girl)
- ✔ **las niñas** *(lahs <u>nee</u>-nyahs)* (the girls)
- ✔ **una niña** *(<u>oo</u>-nah <u>nee</u>-nyah)* (a girl)
- ✔ **unas niñas** *(<u>oo</u>-nahs <u>nee</u>-nyahs)* (some girls)

Look at the **los niños** entry in the preceding list and notice that the translation is plural for both "the boys" and "the children." When you have mixed company (both males and females), you use the male plural article. So **los niños** can mean "boys" or "boys and girls." You follow the same pattern with **unos.**

Okay, okay, so Spanish and English are both vague in places, you say. And Spanish speakers say, sorry, that's the way it is. Languages, like people, all reserve the right to be vague at times.

Make It Two (or More): Plurals

You may not be aware of this, but you already know how to make plurals of Spanish nouns: Simply add *s* to both the article and to the noun.

Spanish is a melodious language. It doesn't like to have two consonants at the end of a word, so it inserts a vowel between them — as in **mujer, mujeres.** So when a noun ends in a consonant, before adding the *s* to turn it into a plural, Spanish inserts an *e.* The following list gives you some examples:

- ✔ **la mujer** *(lah moo-Hehr)* (the woman)
- ✔ **una mujer** *(oo-nah moo-Hehr)* (a woman)
- ✔ **unas mujeres** *(oo-nahs moo-Heh-rehs)* (some women)
- ✔ **el pan** *(ehl pahn)* (the bread)
- ✔ **los panes** *(lohs pah-nehs)* (the breads)
- ✔ **un pan** *(oon pahn)* (a bread)
- ✔ **unos panes** *(oo-nohs pah-nehs)* (some breads)
- ✔ **el canal** *(ehl kah-nahl)* (the channel)
- ✔ **los canales** *(lohs kah-nah-lehs)* (the channels)
- ✔ **un canal** *(oon kah-nahl)* (a channel)
- ✔ **unos canales** *(oo-nohs kah-nah-lehs)* (some channels)
- ✔ **el doctor** *(ehl dohk-tohr)* (the doctor)
- ✔ **los doctores** *(lohs dohk-toh-rehs)* (the doctors)
- ✔ **un doctor** *(oon dohk-tohr)* (a doctor)
- ✔ **unos doctores** *(oo-nohs dohk-toh-rehs)* (some doctors)

Telling Tales with Adjectives

A noun tells you what you're talking about, and a pronoun tells you whom you're talking about. But, adjectives are more fun. They tell you what these things and people are like. Adjectives are the essence of gossip!

When you talk or gossip in Spanish, you're very specific about gender and number. In fact, even adjectives get to show their gender and number.

Suppose that you want to say, "I have a white car." In Spanish you say, **Tengo un carro blanco** (_tehn_-goh oon _kah_-rroh _bvlahn_-koh). Remember, because it ends in _o_, **carro** is masculine. A masculine noun gets a masculine adjective: **blanco** (_bvlahn_-koh).

When you talk about things in the plural, you add the letter _s_ to the adjective to show that you're talking about more than one. So, **blanco** (_bvlahn_-koh) becomes **blancos** (_bvlahn_-kohs), **alta** (_ahl_-tah) becomes **altas** (_ahl_-tahs), and so on. More examples follow:

✔ **Las dos mujeres son altas.** (lahs dohs moo-_Heh_-rehs sohn _ahl_-tahs) (The two women are tall.)

✔ **Ocho hombres altos van en un auto rojo.** (_oh_-choh _ohm_-bvrehs _ahl_-tohs bvahn ehn oon _ahoo_-toh _roh_-Hoh) (Eight tall men go in a red car.)

It's You, You Know: The Tú/Usted Issue

Relationships tend to be more formal in Spanish than in English. If you need to be formal in English, you have to show it by your body movements or the tone of your voice. In Spanish, the distinction between **tú** (too) and **usted** (oos-_tehd_) enables you to introduce this formality right into the language.

In the olden days, English speakers said *thou* and *you*. People said *thou* to their beloved and *you* to their beloved's parents. Anyone listening to a conversation knew whether the speakers were intimate or had a more formal relationship.

Spanish speakers kept this habit. Spanish speakers say **tú** *(too)* as English speakers used to say *thou* and **usted** *(oos-tehd)* to signify a more respectful way of talking to someone, such as a new acquaintance, an older person, or someone they consider to be of higher rank.

Human relations are rigged with feelings. Only you know when you want to be more personal with someone. The beauty of Spanish is that you have a verbal means to manifest these feelings.

At some point in a relationship between people who speak Spanish, a shift occurs from the formal **usted** to the more informal and intimate **tú.** Two people of the same age, the same rank, or the same educational level, or people who want to express a certain intimacy, very soon arrive at a point where they want to talk to each other in a more informal or intimate manner. They use the word **tú** at this point when addressing each other. In Spanish, we call this **tutearse** *(too-teh-ahr-seh),* that is, "to talk **tú.**" Most adults address children using **tú.** These formalities make relationships more graceful and more varied. People in Spanish-speaking places greatly appreciate you being graceful in your speech and your relationships.

On the other hand, if you don't want to have a closer, more intimate relationship with someone, or if you want to keep the relationship more professional and less chummy, you should stick to calling that person **usted.**

Following are some examples of sentences that use **tú** and **usted:**

- ✔ **¿Cómo se llama usted?** *(koh-moh seh yah-mah oos-tehd)* (What's your name? [Respectful])

- ✔ **¿Vas tú con Juan en el auto rojo?** *(bvahs too kohn Hooahn ehn ehl ahoo-toh roh-Hoh)* (Do you go with Juan in the red car? [Friendly, intimate])

- ✔ **Usted tiene una casa muy bella.** *(oos-tehd teeeh-neh oo-nah kah-sah mooy bveh-yah)* (You [singular] have a very beautiful house [Respectful, formal].)

When people in Spain want to address several persons, they use the word **vosotros** *(bvoh-soh-trohs),* which is the plural form of the informal "you." Spanish-speaking Americans almost never use **vosotros.**

One of the main differences between the Spain Spanish way of addressing several people and the Spanish-speaking American one is that in Spanish America, people say **ustedes** *(oos-teh-dehs)* (meaning "you," in the plural — but "they" in conjugation). This **ustedes** can be a formal way of addressing two or more people, or it can be very informal. The situation dictates the difference. Here are some examples:

- ✔ **¿Adónde van ustedes dos?** *(ah dohn-deh bvahn oos-teh-dehs dohs)* (Where are the two of you going?)

  Can be very informal, or formal

- ✔ **¿Tú viajas en el auto?** *(too bveeah-Hahs ehn ehl ahoo-toh)* (Do you travel in the car?)

  Informal

- ✔ **¿A usted le gusta el tango?** *(ah oos-tehd leh goos-tah ehl tahn-goh)* (Do you like the tango?)

  Formal

In written texts, you may find the words **usted** and **ustedes** in their abbreviated forms (**Ud.** for **usted** and **Uds.** for **ustedes**). When you read these abbreviations aloud, you say the whole word.

Chapter 3

Numerical Gumbo: Counting of All Kinds

• •

In This Chapter
▶ Counting to 10
▶ Telling time
▶ Spending money

• •

*N*umbers make the world go round. Or is that money? Well, it's probably both, so this chapter gives you the number and money phrases that you need to get around your world. It also shows you how to tell time and navigate the months of the year.

1, 2, 3: Cardinal Numbers

You can get by with asking for one thing, or more than one thing, or even some things . . . for a while. But eventually you'll want to ask for two things, or ten things, so we show you how to count in Spanish.

Numeral	Number	Pronunciation
1	uno	<u>oo</u>-noh
2	dos	dohs
3	tres	trehs

(continued)

Numeral	Number	Pronunciation
4	cuatro	kooah-troh
5	cinco	seen-koh
6	seis	sehees
7	siete	see-eh-teh
8	ocho	oh-choh
9	nueve	noo-eh-bveh
10	diez	dee-ehs
11	once	ohn-seh
12	doce	doh-seh
13	trece	treh-seh
14	catorce	kah-tohr-seh
15	quince	keen-seh
16	dieciséis	deeeh-see-sehees
17	diecisiete	deeeh-see-seeeh-teh
18	dieciocho	deeeh-seeoh-choh
19	diecinueve	deeeh-see-nooeh-bveh
20	veinte	bveheen-teh
21	veintiuno	bveheen-teeoo-noh
22	veintidós	bveheen-tee-dohs
30	treinta	treheen-tah
31	treinta y uno	treheen-tah ee oo-noh
32	treinta y dos	treheen-tah ee dohs
40	cuarenta	kooah-rehn-tah
41	cuarenta y uno	kooah-rehn-tah ee oo-noh
50	cincuenta	seen-kooehn-tah

Numeral	Number	Pronunciation
51	cincuenta y uno	seen-koo<u>ehn</u>-tah ee <u>oo</u>-noh
60	sesenta	seh-<u>sehn</u>-tah
61	sesenta y uno	seh-<u>sehn</u>-tah ee <u>oo</u>-noh
70	setenta	seh-<u>tehn</u>-tah
71	setenta y uno	seh-<u>sehn</u>-tah ee <u>oo</u>-noh
80	ochenta	oh-<u>chehn</u>-tah
81	ochenta y uno	oh-<u>chehn</u>-tah ee <u>oo</u>-noh
90	noventa	noh-<u>bvehn</u>-tah
91	noventa y uno	noh-<u>bvehn</u>-tah ee <u>oo</u>-noh
100	cien	see-<u>ehn</u>
500	quinientos	kee-nee<u>ehn</u>-tohs
1000	mil	meel

Discovering Ordinal Numbers

When given directions, you hear many phrases describing things like the third block to the left or the fourth floor. So ordinal numbers are extremely useful. Here are the first ten:

- ✔ **primero** *(pree-<u>meh</u>-roh)* (first)
- ✔ **segundo** *(seh-<u>goon</u>-doh)* (second)
- ✔ **tercero** *(tehr-<u>seh</u>-roh)* (third)
- ✔ **cuarto** *(koo<u>ahr</u>-toh)* (fourth)
- ✔ **quinto** *(<u>keen</u>-toh)* (fifth)
- ✔ **sexto** *(<u>sehks</u>-toh)* (sixth)
- ✔ **séptimo** *(<u>sehp</u>-tee-moh)* (seventh)
- ✔ **octavo** *(ohk-<u>tah</u>-bvoh)* (eighth)

✔ **noveno** (*noh-bveh-noh*) (ninth)

✔ **décimo** (*deh-see-moh*) (tenth)

Here are some phrases to help you practice using ordinal numbers:

✔ **Vivo en el octavo piso.** (*bvee-bvoh ehn ehl ohk-tah-bvoh pee-soh*) (I live on the eighth floor.)

✔ **En el primer piso hay una florería.** (*ehn ehl pree-mehr pee-soh ahy oo-nah floh-reh-reeah*) (On the first floor, there is a flower shop.)

✔ **La terraza está en el décimonoveno piso.** (*lah teh-rrah-sah ehs-tah ehn ehl deh-see-moh-noh-bveh-noh pee-soh*) (The terrace is on the nine-teenth floor.)

Telling Time

All countries may have their own sense of time, but you still need to know how to tell it.

You can tell time

¿Qué hora es? (*keh oh-rah ehs*) (What time is it?) is a question you may need to ask often. To tell time, just add the minutes to the hour, like you do in English. Check out these phrases to see how it works:

✔ **Son las ocho cuarenta y cinco.** (*sohn lahs oh-choh kooah-rehn-tah ee seen-koh*) (It's 8:45.)

✔ **Son las veinte y treinta horas.** (*sohn lahs bve-heen-teh ee treheen-tah oh-rahs*) (It's 8:30 p.m. [Literally: It's twenty and thirty hours.])

✔ **Voy a las diez de la mañana.** (*bvohy ah lahs deeehs deh lah mah-nyah-nah*) (I'm going at ten o'clock in the morning.)

✔ **Llega a las nueve de la noche.** (*yeh-gah ah lahs nooeh-bveh deh lah noh-cheh*) (He arrives at nine o'clock in the evening.)

- ✔ **Vengo a la una y cuarto.** (*bvehn-goh ah lah oo-nah ee kooahr-toh*) (I'm coming at a quarter past one.)

- ✔ **Un cuarto para las dos llovió.** (*oon kooahr-toh pah-rah lahs dohs yoh-bveeoh*) (It rained at a quarter to two.)

- ✔ **Son diez para las once.** (*sohn deeehs pah-rah lahs ohn-seh.*) (It's ten to eleven.)

These phrases help you set the time and place when you're ready to go out on the town:

- ✔ **¿a qué hora?** (*ah keh oh-rah*) (at what time?)

- ✔ **¿cuándo comienza?** (*kooahn-doh koh-meeehn-sah*) (when does it start?)

- ✔ **¿hasta qué hora?** (*ahs-tah keh oh-rah*) (until what time?)

Words to Know

la hora	lah oh-rah	the hour
el minuto	ehl mee-noo-toh	the minute
el segundo	ehl seh-goon-doh	the second
el cuarto	ehl kooahr-toh	the quarter
el medio	ehl meh-deeoh	the half
mediodía	meh-deeoh-deeah	noon
medianoche	meh-deeah-noh-cheh	midnight
la tarde	lah tahr-deh	the afternoon
la noche	lah noh-cheh	the night

But are you on time?

The following list contains phrases for when you want
to schedule something:

- **a la hora** *(ah lah oh-rah)* (on time)
- **anda atrasado** *(ahn-dah ah-trah-sah-doh)* ([it] is
running late)
- **viene adelantado** *(bveeeh-neh ah-deh-lahn-tah-
doh)* ([it] is coming early)
- **el horario** *(ehl oh-rah-reeoh)* (the schedule)
- **es temprano** *(ehs tehm-prah-noh)* (it's early)
[time]
- **es tarde** *(ehs tahr-deh)* (it's late) [time]
- **la tarde** *(lah tahr-deh)* (the afternoon)

The word **tarde** *(tahr-deh)* has different
meanings, depending on whether you use
the article.

Sometimes, the posted schedule for a bus, train, or
plane isn't up-to-date and you may need to ask someone about it. Here are some responses you may hear:

- **Hay que esperar, está atrasado.** *(ahy keh ehs-
peh-rahr ehs-tah ah-trah-sah-doh)* (One has to
wait; it's late.)
- **El vuelo llegó adelantado.** *(ehl bvooeh-loh yeh-
goh ah-deh-lahn-tah-doh)* (The flight came early.)
- **El reloj está adelantado.** *(ehl reh-lohH ehs-tah
ah-deh-lahn-tah-doh)* (The clock is fast.)
- **El bus va adelantado.** *(ehl bvoos bvah ah-deh-
lahn-tah-doh)* (The bus goes early.)
- **El tren va a llegar a la hora.** *(ehl trehn bvah ah
yeh-gahr ah lah oh-rah)* (The train will arrive on
time.)
- **Esperan porque va a llegar tarde.** *(ehs-peh-rahn
pohr-keh bvah a yeh-gahr tahr-deh)* (They're waiting because it will arrive late.)

✔ **El bus viene a la hora.** *(ehl bvoos bveeeh-neh ah lah oh-rah)* (The bus comes on time.)

If you're running late, you may say

✔ **Es tarde; ya son las ocho.** *(ehs tahr-deh; yah sohn lahs oh-choh)* (It's late; it's already eight o'clock.)

✔ **Estoy atrasado; ya es mediodía.** *(ehs-tohy ah-trah-sah-doh; yah ehs meh-deeoh-deeah)* (I'm late; it's already noon.)

✔ **Me tengo que apurar, es medianoche.** *(meh tehn-goh keh ah-poo-rahr, ehs meh-deeah-noh-cheh)* (I have to hurry; it's midnight.)

✔ **Un minuto, por favor.** *(oon mee-noo-toh, pohr fah-bvohr)* (One minute, please.)

✔ **Un segundo, por favor.** *(ooh seh-goon-doh, pohr fah-bvohr)* (One second, please.)

✔ **Un momento, por favor.** *(oon moh-mehn-toh pohr fah-bvohr)* (One moment, please.)

If you're approximating the time of day, you say

✔ **Es tarde.** *(ehs tahr-deh)* (It's late.)

✔ **Es temprano.** *(ehs tehm-prah-noh)* (It's early.)

✔ **Estoy atrasado.** *(ehs-tohy ah-trah-sah-doh)* (I'm late.)

Days, Months, Seasons

Okay, so days and months aren't really numbers, but they're a way of measuring time. The following sections give you what you need to know.

What day is it?

Here are the days of the week in Spanish:

✔ **lunes** *(loo-nehs)* (Monday)

✔ **martes** *(mahr-tehs)* (Tuesday)

✔ **miércoles** *(meeehr-koh-lehs)* (Wednesday)

✔ **jueves** *(Hooeh-bvehs)* (Thursday)

✔ **viernes** *(bveeehr-nehs)* (Friday)

✔ **sábado** *(sah-bvah-doh)* (Saturday)

✔ **domingo** *(doh-meen-goh)* (Sunday)

These phrases may come in handy when talking about the day of the week:

✔ **La clase va a ser el martes.** *(lah klah-seh bvah a sehr ehl mahr-tehs)* (The class will be held on Tuesday.)

✔ **No puedo ir hasta el miércoles.** *(noh pooeh-doh eer ahs-tah ehl meeehr-koh-lehs)* (I can't go until Wednesday.)

✔ **Va a llegar el viernes.** *(bvah ah yeh-gahr ehl bveeehr-nes)* (He's going to arrive on Friday.)

✔ **Me voy el domingo.** *(meh bvohy ehl doh-meen-goh)* (I'm leaving on Sunday.)

Sometimes, you also need to state the approximate time, as in the following phrases:

✔ **la semana entrante** *(lah seh-mah-nah ehn-trahn-teh)* (the next week [Literally: the week entering])

✔ **la semana próxima** *(lah seh-mah-nah proh-ksee-mah)* (next week)

✔ **la semana que viene** *(lah seh-mah-nah keh bveeeh-neh)* (next week [Literally: the week that comes])

✔ **La semana entrante va a venir en avión.** *(lah seh-mah-nah ehn-trahn-teh bvah ah bveh-neer ehn ah-bveeohn)* (She/He'll come by air next week.)

✔ **La semana siguiente es buena fecha.** *(lah seh-mah-nah see-gheeehn-teh ehs bvoo eh-nah feh-chah)* (The following week is a good date.)

Living month to month

Note that in Spanish, the names of the months don't begin with a capital letter, as they do in English:

- ✔ **enero** *(eh-neh-roh)* (January)
- ✔ **febrero** *(feh-bvreh-roh)* (February)
- ✔ **marzo** *(mahr-soh)* (March)
- ✔ **abril** *(ah-bvreel)* (April)
- ✔ **mayo** *(mah-yoh)* (May)
- ✔ **junio** *(Hoo-neeoh)* (June)
- ✔ **julio** *(Hoo-leeoh)* (July)
- ✔ **agosto** *(ah-gohs-toh)* (August)
- ✔ **septiembre** *(sehp-teeehm-breh)* (September)
- ✔ **octubre** *(ohk-too-bvreh)* (October)
- ✔ **noviembre** *(noh-bveeehm-breh)* (November)
- ✔ **diciembre** *(dee-seeehm-breh)* (December)

You may find yourself needing phrases like the ones in the following examples when talking about the months:

- ✔ **En enero voy a ir a Colombia.** *(ehn eh-neh-roh bvoy ah eer a koh-lohm-bveeah)* (In January, I'm going to go to Colombia.)
- ✔ **Vuelvo de España en marzo.** *(bvoo-ehl-bvoh de ehs-pah-nyah ehn mahr-soh)* (I return from Spain in March.)
- ✔ **El viaje es de julio a diciembre.** *(ehl bveeah-Heh ehs deh Hoo-leeoh ah dee-seeehm-bvreh)* (The trip is from July to December.)
- ✔ **La estación de lluvias es de mayo a noviembre.** *(lah ehs-tah-seeohn deh yoo-bveeahs ehs deh mah-yoh ah noh-bveeehm-bvreh)* (The rainy season is from May to November.)

Words to Know

otoño	oh-_toh_-nyoh	autumn
verano	bvehr-_ah_-noh	summer
primavera	pree-mah-_veh_-rah	spring
invierno	een-bveee_ehr_-noh	winter
la Seca	lah _seh_-kah	the dry season
la de Las Lluvias	lah deh lahs _yoo_-bveeahs	the rainy season

Counting Your Money

In the following sections, you discover all the money-handling knowledge that you need to use with all those Spanish-speakers.

Carrying cash

Here are a few cash-carrying terms you may need:

- **dinero en efectivo** (dee-_neh_-roh ehn eh-fehk-_tee_-bvoh) (money in cash)
- **en billetes** (ehn bvee-_yeh_-tehs) (in bills)
- **en monedas** (ehn moh-_neh_-dahs) (in coins)
- **una moneda de oro** (_oo_-nah moh-_neh_-dah deh _oh_-roh) (a gold coin)
- **la moneda de plata** (lah moh-_neh_-dah deh _plah_-tah) (the silver coin)

The following little cash-carrying phrases also may come in handy:

✔ **¿Traes algún dinero?** *(trah-ehs ahl-goon dee-neh-roh)* (Do you have any money?)

✔ **¿Tienes dinero en efectivo?** *(teeeh-nehs dee-neh-roh ehn eh-fehk-tee-bvoh)* (Do you have cash?)

✔ **¿Tiene una moneda de cincuenta centavos?** *(teeeh-neh oo-nah moh-neh-dah deh seen-kooehn-tah sehn-tah-bvohs)* (Do you have a fifty-cent coin?)

✔ **No tenemos monedas.** *(noh teh-neh-mohs moh-neh-dahs)* (We have no coins.)

✔ **Necesitan dos monedas de diez centavos.** *(neh-seh-see-tahn dohs moh-neh-dahs deh deeehs sehn-tah-bvohs)* (They need two ten-cent coins.)

✔ **Pagamos con dos billetes de veinte pesos.** *(pah-gah-mohs kohn dohs bvee-yeh-tehs deh bveheen-teh peh-sohs)* (We paid with two twenty-peso bills.)

✔ **Aquí tiene un billete de cien colones.** *(ah-kee teeeh-neh oon bvee-yeh-teh deh seeehn koh-loh-nehs)* (Here you have a hundred colon bill.)

Words to Know

algún	ahl-goon	some
el dinero	ehl dee-neh-roh	the money
el billete	ehl bvee-yeh-teh	the bill
la moneda	lah moh-neh-dah	the coin

ATMs

Some ATMs have both Spanish and English. Just in case yours doesn't have the English display, here are the sentences that you see in the order in which they appear:

✔ **Introduzca su tarjeta por favor.** *(een-troh-doos-kah soo tahr-Heh-tah pohr-fah-bvohr)* (Insert your card, please.)

✔ **Por favor teclee su número confidencial.** *(pohr fah-bvohr teh-kleh-eh soo noo-meh-roh kohn-fee-dehn-seeahl)* (Please type your PIN.)

At this point, you have to press the button that reads **Continuar** *(kohn-tee-nooahr)* (Continue; keep going.) After you press the button, the following choices appear:

✔ **Retiro en efectivo** *(reh-tee-roh ehn eh-fehk-tee-bvoh)* (Cash withdrawal)

   If you choose cash withdrawal, these other choices come up:

   Tarjeta de crédito *(tahr-Heh-tah deh kreh-dee-toh)* (Credit card)

   Cuenta de cheques *(kooehn-tah deh cheh-kehs)* (Checking account)

   Débito/inversiones *(deh-bvee-toh/een-bvehr-seeoh-nehs)* (Debit/investments)

✔ **Consulta de saldo** *(kohn-sool-tah deh sahl-doh)* (Checking your balance)

If you're slow about pressing those buttons, these signs come up:

✔ **¿Requiere más tiempo?** *(reh-keeeh-reh mahs teeehm-poh?)* Do you need more time?

✔ **Sí/No** *(see/noh)* (Yes/No)

If you press yes, you go back to the previous screen. When this happens, choose **cuenta de cheques** *(kooehn-tah deh cheh-kehs),* which gives you choices for cash:

✔ 100, 200, 300, 400, 500, 1,000, 1,500

✔ **¿Otra cantidad?** *(oh-trah kahn-tee-dahd)* (Another amount?)

Press the key for the desired amount, and your money comes out. Then the following messages come up:

- ✔ **Entregado** *(ehn-treh-gah-doh)* (Delivered)

- ✔ **Saldo** *(sahl-doh)* (Balance)

- ✔ **Por favor tome su dinero** *(pohr fah-bvohr toh-meh soo dee-neh-roh)* (Please take your money)

Words to Know

introducir	een-troh-doo-seer	insert
retiro	reh-tee-roh	withdrawal
saldo	sahl-doh	balance
cuenta	koo-ehn-tah	account
débito	deh-bvee-toh	debit
cantidad	kahn-tee-dahd	quantity; amount
entregar	ehn-treh-gahr	to deliver

Credit cards

Credit cards are very convenient, but they aren't accepted everywhere. Here are some phrases you may need to know:

- ✔ **¿Aceptan tarjetas de crédito?** *(ah-sehp-tahn tahr-Heh-tahs deh kreh-dee-toh)* Do you take credit cards?

- ✔ **Aquí tiene mi tarjeta.** *(ah-kee teeeh-neh mee tahr-Heh-tah)* Here is my card.

- ✔ **Un momento, ya vuelvo con su recibo.** *(oon moh-mehn-toh, yah bvooehl-bvoh kohn soo reh-see-bvoh)* One moment, I'm coming back with your receipt.

✔ **Firme aquí, por favor.** (*feer-meh ah-kee, pohr fah-bvohr*) Sign here, please.

✔ **Aquí tiene su tarjeta y su recibo. Gracias.** (*ah-kee teeeh-neh soo tahr-Heh-tah ee soo reh-see-bvoh grah-seeahs*) Here's your card and your receipt. Thank you.

Words to Know

servir	sehr-bveer	to serve; to be of service
la tarjeta	lah tahr-Heh-tah	the card
el recibo	ehl reh-see-bvoh	the receipt
firmar	feer-mahr	to sign
la autorización	lah ahoo-toh-ree-sah-seeohn	the authorization
la ventanilla	lah bvehn-tah-nee-yah	the little window
la identificación	lah ee-dehn-tee-fee-kah-seeohn	the identification

Exchanging your dollars

Each country has its own currency. When you travel, you need to use the local currency to make your transactions, so you'll have to exchange your dollars.

In Spanish, to change and to exchange are expressed with the same verb, **cambiar** (*kahm-bvee-ahr*). It's a regular verb, so see Chapter 2 for the conjugation.

Knowing these phrases comes in handy when trying to find a place to exchange money:

- ✔ **¿Dónde puedo cambiar dólares?** *(dohn-deh pooeh-doh kahm-bveeahr doh-lah-rehs)* (Where can I exchange dollars?)

- ✔ **¿Dónde encuentro una casa de cambio?** *(dohn-deh ehn-kooehn-troh oo-nah kah-sah deh kahm-bveeoh)* (Where can I find a place to exchange money?)

- ✔ **La casa de cambio te puede cambiar tus dólares.** *(lah kah-sah deh kahm-bveeoh teh pooeh-deh kahm-bveeahr toos doh-lah-rehs)* (The exchange bureau can exchange your dollars.)

- ✔ **En el banco cambian dólares.** *(ehn ehl bvahn-koh kahm-bveeahn doh-lah-rehs)* (At the bank you can exchange [your dollars].)

- ✔ **En esa ventanilla cambian monedas.** *(ehn eh-sah bvehn-tah-nee-yah kahm-bveeahn moh-neh-dahs)* (At that window, they change coins.)

The person who lends or exchanges money is called **el cambista** *(ehl kahm-bvees-tah)* (money changer).

After you're at the **casa de cambio,** you may need to know these phrases:

- ✔ **Quiero cambiar dólares por bolívares.** *(keeeh-roh kahm-bveeahr doh-lah-rehs pohr bvoh-lee-bvah-rehs)* (I want to exchange dollars for bolivars.)

- ✔ **¿A cuánto está el dólar americano?** *(ah kooahn-toh ehs-tah ehl doh-lahr ah-meh-ree-kah-noh)* (What's the exchange for the U.S. dollar?)

- ✔ **¿A la compra o a la venta?** *(ah lah kohm-prah oh ah lah bvehn-tah)* (Buying or selling?)

- ✔ **¿Me cambia cien, por favor?** *(meh kahm-bveeah seeehn pohr fah-bvohr)* (Will you exchange me one hundred, please?)

✔ **Cómo no, aquí tiene el recibo, aquí el dinero.** (_koh_-moh noh, ah-_kee_-tee_eh_-neh ehl reh-_see_-bvoh ah-_kee_ ehl dee-_neh_-roh) (Sure, here's the receipt, here's the money.)

✔ **Es muy alta la comisión con que cambian.** (ehs mooy _ahl_-tah la koh-mee-see_ohn_ kohn keh _kahm_-bveeahn) (The commission they charge for the exchange is too high.)

Chapter 4

Making New Friends and Enjoying Small Talk

• •

In This Chapter

▶ Introducing yourself

▶ Asking questions

▶ Chatting about the weather and family

• •

*M*eeting new people and getting to know them can be stressful, especially when you have to converse in a language that isn't your own. This chapter helps you make small talk with your Spanish-speaking friends and neighbors.

Hello! Greetings and Introductions

As you begin a relationship, Latin Americans believe that keeping a certain distance is best. Only when you already know the person should you use the friendlier, informal phrases.

Formal introductions

Here's a possible formal introduction that a person may have as he approaches a table at a sidewalk cafe with a person already sitting there.

✔ **Pedro: ¿Me permite?** *(meh pehr-mee-teh)* (May I?)

✔ **Jane: Sí, ¡adelante!** *(see, ah-deh-lahn-teh)* (Yes, [go] ahead!)

✔ **Pedro: Buenas tardes. Me llamo Pedro García Fernández.** *(bvooeh-nahs tahr-dehs meh yah-moh peh-droh gahr-seeah fehr-nahn-dehs)* (Good afternoon. My name is Pedro García Fernández.)

✔ **Jane: Mucho gusto, señor García.** *(moo-choh goos-toh seh-nyohr gahr-seeah)* (Nice to meet you, Mr. García.)

✔ **Pedro: Y usted ¿cómo se llama?** *(ee oos-tehd koh-moh seh yah-mah)* (And what's your name?)

✔ **Jane: Me llamo Jane Wells.** *(meh yah-moh Jane Wells)* (My name is Jane Wells.)

✔ **Pedro: Mucho gusto.** *(moo-choh goos-toh)* (A pleasure.)

Here's a way that you can introduce two people other than yourself:

✔ **Pepe: Buenas tardes. ¿El señor Kendall?** *(bvooeh-nahs tahr-dehs ehl seh-nyohr Kendall)* (Good afternoon. Mr. Kendall?)

✔ **Mr. Kendall: Sí, me llamo Kendall.** *(see meh yah-moh Kendall)* (Yes, my name is Kendall.)

✔ **Pepe: Permítame que le presente al señor Fernando Quintana Martínez.** *(pehr-mee-tah-me keh leh preh-sehn-teh ahl seh-nyohr fehr-nahn-doh keen-tah-nah mahr-tee-nehs)* (Allow me to introduce Mr. Fernando Quintana Martínez.)

✔ **Mr. Kendall: Mucho gusto.** *(moo-choh goos-toh)* (A pleasure.)

✔ **Pepe: Y esta es la señora Lucía Sánchez de Quintana.** *(ee ehs-tah ehs lah seh-nyoh-rah loo-seeah sahn-ches deh keen-tah-nah)* (And this is Mrs. Lucía Sánchez de Quintana.)

✔ **Mr. Kendall: Mucho gusto, señora.** *(moo-choh goos-toh seh-nyoh-rah)* (A pleasure, ma'am.)

Say you want to formally greet someone you work with:

> ✔ **Sra. Salinas: Buenos días, Sr. Rivera. ¿Cómo está?** *(bvooeh-nohs deeahs seh-nyohr ree-veh-rah koh-moh ehs-tah)* (Good morning, Mr. Rivera. How are you?)
>
> ✔ **Sr. Rivera: Muy bien. ¿Y Ud.?** *(mooy bveeehn ee oos-tehd)* (Very well. And you?)
>
> ✔ **Sra. Salinas: Bien, gracias.** *(bveeehn, grah-seeahs)* (Well, thank you.)

If you're being introduced to a very important or famous person, you want to be especially formal. You may want to use the following examples:

> ✔ **¿Me permite presentarle a . . . .?** *(meh pehr-mee-teh preh-sehn-tahr-leh ah)* (May I introduce. . . .?)
>
> ✔ **Es un gusto conocerle.** *(ehs oon goos-toh koh-noh-sehr-leh)* (It's a pleasure to meet you.)
>
> ✔ **El gusto es mío.** *(ehl goos-toh ehs meeoh)* (The pleasure is mine.)

Informal introductions

Here's how two teenagers may informally introduce themselves to each other:

> ✔ **John: ¡Hola! ¿Cómo te llamas?** *(oh-lah! koh-moh teh yah-mahs)* (Hi! What's your name?)
>
> ✔ **Julia: Me llamo Julia. ¿Y tú?** *(meh yah-moh Hoo-leeah ee too)* (My name is Julia. And yours?)
>
> ✔ **John: Yo me llamo John.** *(yoh meh yah-moh John)* (My name is John.)

And if they want to greet each other a few days later, they can say:

> ✔ **John: Buenos días. ¿Qué tal?** *(bvooeh-nohs deeahs keh tahl)* (Good morning. How are things?)

> ✔ **Julia: ¡Ah, hola, John! ¿Cómo estás?** *(ah oh-lah john koh-moh ehs-tahs)* (Ah, hello, John! How are you?)
>
> ✔ **John: Bien. ¿Y tú?** *(bveeehn ee tooh)* (Well. And you?)
>
> ✔ **Julia: Bien.** *(bveeehn)* (Well.)

Small-Talk Verbs

When you're meeting someone new and making small talk, you use a few verbs quite frequently. We've conjugated the irregular verbs in the following sections. If you need to jog your memory on how to conjugate the regular verbs, check out Chapter 2.

Llamarse: Calling

The verb **llamarse** *(yah-mar-seh)* (to call) is a regular **-ar** verb; however, the **se** at the end of it tells you that the verb is reflexive, which makes it irregular, too (nobody said grammar was easy). Table 4-1 conjugates this verb for you. And in case your memory needs to jog a little, a *reflexive verb* is one that acts on the noun (or object) of the sentence. For instance, the sentence **yo me llamo** *(yo meh yah-moh)* literally means "I call myself." In this case, "I" is the subject of the sentence and "call myself" reflects back to "I." Anytime you see the *se* at the end of a verb, you simply put the reflexive pronoun (*me* in the example sentence) in front of the verb.

Table 4-1	Llamarse
Conjugation	*Pronunciation*
yo me llamo	yoh meh yah-moh
tú te llamas	too teh yah-mahs
él, ella, ello, uno, usted se llama	ehl, eh-yah, eh-yo, oo-noh, oos-tehd seh yah-mah

Conjugation	Pronunciation
nosotros nos llamamos	noh-<u>soh</u>-trohs nohs yah-<u>mah</u>-mohs
vosotros os llamáis	bvoh-<u>soh</u>-trohs ohs yah-<u>mahees</u>
ellos, ellas, ustedes se llaman	<u>eh</u>-yohs, <u>eh</u>-yahs, oos-<u>teh</u>-dehs seh <u>yah</u>-mahn

Ser: Being

Ser *(sehr)* (to be) refers to a kind of permanent being, like the fact that you are you. The word also refers to all things that are expected to be permanent, such as places, countries, and certain conditions or states of being, such as shape, profession, nationality, and place of origin:

- ✔ **Soy mujer.** *(sohy moo-<u>Hehr</u>)* (I'm a woman.)

- ✔ **Soy canadiense.** *(sohy kah-nah-dee-<u>ehn</u>-seh)* (I'm Canadian.)

- ✔ **Soy de Winnipeg.** *(sohy de Winnipeg)* (I'm from Winnipeg.)

- ✔ **Ellos son muy altos.** *(<u>eh</u>-yohs sohn mooy <u>ahl</u>-tohs)* (They're very tall.)

- ✔ **¿Ustedes son uruguayos?** *(oos-<u>teh</u>-dehs sohn oo-roo-<u>gooah</u>-yohs)* (Are you [formal] Uruguayan?)

- ✔ **Ella es maestra.** *(<u>eh</u>-yah ehs mah-<u>ehs</u>-trah)* (She's a teacher.)

- ✔ **Eres muy bella.** *(<u>eh</u>-rehs mooy <u>bveh</u>-yah)* (You are very beautiful.)

- ✔ **Eres muy gentil.** *(<u>eh</u>-rehs mooy Hehn-<u>teel</u>)* (You are very kind.)

Table 4-2 shows the conjugation of **ser**.

Table 4-2	Ser
Conjugation	*Pronunciation*
yo soy	yoh <u>soh</u>y
tú eres	too <u>eh</u>-rehs
él, ella, ello, uno, usted es	ehl, <u>eh</u>-yah, <u>eh</u>-yoh, <u>oo</u>-noh, <u>oos</u>-tehd, ehs
nosotros somos	noh-<u>soh</u>-trohs <u>soh</u>-mohs
vosotros sois	bvoh-<u>soh</u>-trohs <u>soh</u>ees
ellos, ellas, ustedes son	<u>eh</u>-yohs, <u>eh</u>-yahs, oos-<u>teh</u>-dehs sohn

You use **ser** to describe where you live:

> ✔ **Roberto: Jane, ¿de qué ciudad es?** *(Jane deh keh seeoo-<u>dahd</u> ehs)* (Jane, what city are you from?)

> ✔ **Jane: Soy de New Berlin, en el estado de Nueva York.** *(sohy deh New Berlin ehn ehl ehs-<u>tah</u>-doh deh noo<u>eh</u>-bvah yohrk)* (I'm from New Berlin in New York State.)

> ✔ **Roberto: ¿Es esa una ciudad grande?** *(ehs <u>eh</u>-sah <u>oo</u>-nah seeoo-<u>dahd</u> <u>grahn</u>-deh)* (Is that a very large city?)

> ✔ **Jane: Es un pueblo chico, pero muy bonito.** *(ehs oon poo<u>eh</u>-bvloh <u>chee</u>-koh <u>peh</u>-roh mooy bvoh-<u>nee</u>-toh)* (It's a small town, but it's very nice.)

> ✔ **Roberto: Bueno, esta es también una ciudad chica.** *(bvoo<u>eh</u>-noh <u>ehs</u>-tah ehs tahm-bvee<u>ehn</u> <u>oo</u>-nah seeoo-<u>dahd</u> <u>chee</u>-kah)* (Well, this is also a small city.)

✔ **Jane: ¡Para nada!, es bastante grande.** *(pah-rah nah-dah ehs bvahs-tahn-teh grahn-deh)* (Not at all, it's quite big.)

Words to Know

chico	chee-koh	little; small
grande	grahn-deh	big; large
bastante	bvahs-tahn-teh	quite; enough

Ser is also an important verb for finding out information:

✔ **Esperanza: ¿Es bueno el hotel Paraíso?** *(ehs bvooeh-noh ehl oh-tehl pah-rahee-soh)* (Is the hotel Paraíso any good?)

✔ **Esteban: Sí, es un buen hotel.** *(see ehs oon bvooehn oh-tehl)* (Yes, it's a good hotel.)

✔ **Esperanza: ¿Es caro?** *(ehs kah-roh)* (Is it expensive?)

✔ **Esteban: Es un poco caro.** *(ehs oon poh-koh kah-roh)* (It's a little expensive.)

✔ **Esperanza: ¿Es grande?** *(ehs grahn-deh)* (Is it big?)

✔ **Esteban: No, no es muy grande.** *(noh noh ehs mooy grahn-deh)* (No, it's not very big.)

✔ **Esperanza: ¿Es un problema llamar allí?** *(ehs oon proh-bvleh-mah yah-mahr ah-yee)* (Is it a problem to call there?)

✔ **Esteban: No, no es ningún problema.** *(noh noh ehs neen-goon proh-bvleh-mah)* (No, it's no problem.)

Words to Know

buen	bvooehn	good (male)
bueno	bvooeh-noh	good (male)
buena	bvooeh-nah	good (female)
caro	kah-roh	expensive
poco	poh-koh	a bit; small amount
ningún	neen-goon	none

Estar: The second being

When you're talking about a state of being that isn't permanent — such as being someplace (you won't be there forever), or being some temporary way (being ill, for instance) — you use the verb **estar** *(ehs-tahr)*. So in Spanish, it isn't "To be or not to be," but "To be forever (**ser**) or not forever (**estar**)." Check out Table 4-3 for the conjugation.

Table 4-3	Estar
Conjugation	*Pronunciation*
yo estoy	yoh ehs-tohy
tú estás	too ehs-tahs
él, ella, ello, uno, usted está	ehl, eh-yah, eh-yoh, oo-noh, oos-tehd ehs-tah
nosotros estamos	noh-soh-trohs ehs-tah-mohs
vosotros estáis	bvoh-soh-trohs ehs-tahees
ellos, ellas, unos, ustedes están	eh-yohs, eh-yahs, oo-nohs, oos-teh-dehs ehs-tahn

Here's a dialog to help you practice this new way of being, the one that isn't forever:

✔ **Guillermo: ¿Cómo están ustedes?** *(koh-moh ehs-tahn oos-teh-dehs)* (How are you?)

✔ **Sra. Valdés: Estamos muy bien, gracias.** *(ehs-tah-mohs mooy bveeehn grah-seeahs)* (We're very well, thank you.)

✔ **Guillermo: ¿Están de paseo?** *(ehs-tahn deh pah-seh-oh)* (Are you talking a walk?)

✔ **Sra. Valdés: Estamos de vacaciones.** *(ehs-tah-mohs deh bvah-kah-seeoh-nehs)* (We're on vacation.)

✔ **Guillermo: ¿Están contentos?** *(ehs-tahn kohn-tehn-tohs)* (Are you content?)

✔ **Sra. Valdés: Estamos muy felices.** *(ehs-tah-mohs mooy feh-lee-sehs)* (We're very happy.)

✔ **Guillermo: ¿Cómo está su hija?** *(koh-moh ehs-tah soo ee-Hah)* (How is your daughter?)

✔ **Sra. Valdés: Más o menos, no está muy feliz.** *(mahs oh meh-nohs noh ehs-tah mooy feh-lees)* (So-so, she's not very happy.)

Or for another temporary use of **estar,** try this dialogue:

✔ **Renata: ¿Está libre este baño?** *(ehs-tah lee-bvreh ehs-teh bvah-nyoh)* (Is the bathroom free?)

✔ **Elena: No, está ocupado.** *(noh ehs-tah oh-koo-pah-doh)* (No, it's taken.)

✔ **Renata: ¿Está libre el otro baño?** *(ehs-tah lee-bvreh ehl oh-troh bvah-nyoh)* (Is the other bathroom free?)

✔ **Elena: Sí, está libre.** *(see ehs-tah lee-bvreh)* (Yes, it's free.)

Words to Know

el paseo	ehl pah-<u>seh</u>-oh	the walk
contento	kohn-<u>tehn</u>-toh	content; satisfied
feliz	feh-<u>lees</u>	happy
libre	<u>lee</u>-bvreh	free
ocupado	oh-koo-<u>pah</u>-doh	occupied; busy
este	<u>ehs</u>-teh	this one
otro	<u>oh</u>-troh	the other one

Hablar: Speaking

Another verb you need to know about is **hablar** *(ah-bvlahr)* (to speak; to talk). You'll be happy to know that **hablar** is a regular -**ar** verb.

In this conversation, two people talk about talking:

- ✔ **Kathleen: ¿María habla mucho?** *(mah-<u>reeah</u> ah-bvlah <u>moo</u>-choh)* (Does María talk a lot?)

- ✔ **Lorenzo: Sí, le encanta hablar.** *(see leh ehn-<u>kahn</u>-tah ah-bvlahr)* (Yes, she loves to talk.)

- ✔ **Kathleen: Yo hablo mal el español.** *(yoh ah-bvloh mahl ehl ehs-pah-<u>nyohl</u>)* (I speak Spanish badly.)

- ✔ **Lorenzo: ¡Por el contrario, lo habla muy bien!** *(pohr ehl kohn-<u>trah</u>-reeoh loh ah-bvlah mooy bvee<u>ehn</u>)* (On the contrary, you speak it very well!)

Words to Know

mucho	moo-choh	a lot; much
difícil	dee-fee-seel	difficult; hard
fácil	fah-seel	easy
la lengua	lah lehn-gooah	the language (Literally: the tongue)
el idioma	ehl ee-dee-oh-mah	the language
gustar	goos-tahr	to like

Hablar is useful for finding out what languages you speak in common:

- ✔ **Antonia: ¿Habla usted español?** *(ah-blah oos-tehd ehs-pah-nyol)* (Do you speak Spanish?)

- ✔ **Reynaldo: Sí. ¿Qué idiomas habla usted?** *(see keh ee-dee-oh-mahs ah-blah oos-tehd)* (Yes. What languages do you speak?)

- ✔ **Antonia: Yo hablo inglés y francés.** *(yoh ah-bvloh een-glehs ee frahn-sehs)* (I speak English and French.)

- ✔ **Reynaldo: Es muy difícil hablar inglés?** *(ehs mooy dee-fee-seel ah-blahr een-glehs)* (Is it very difficult to speak English?)

- ✔ **Antonia: No, ¡es muy fácil!** *(noh, ehs mooy fah-seel)* (No, it's very easy!)

- ✔ **Reynaldo: ¿Y es difícil hablar francés?** *(ee ehs dee-fee-seel ah-bvlahr frahn-sehs)* (And is it difficult to speak French?)

- ✔ **Antonia: No, no es en absoluto difícil.** *(noh noh ehs ehn ahb-soh-loo-toh dee-fee-seel)* (No, it's not difficult all.)

- **Reynaldo: A mí me gusta mucho hablar español.** *(ah mee meh goos-tah moo-choh ah-bvlahr ehs-pah-nyohl)* (I like to speak Spanish.)

- **Antonia: A mí también.** *(ah mee tahm-bveeehn)* (So do I.)

Words to Know

Ser de aquí	sehr deh ah-kee	To belong to this place; to live here
¿Cómo le va?	koh-moh leh bvah	How are you doing?
¿Cómo van las cosas?	koh-moh bvahn lahs koh-sahs	How are things [going]?
¿Cómo está usted?	koh-moh ehs-tah oos-tehd	How are you? (formal)
¿Cómo estás?	koh-moh ehs-tahs	How are you? (informal)
¿Qué tal?	keh tahl	How are things [Literally: How such]?
Más o menos	mahs oh meh-nohs	So-so [Literally: More or less]
¿Quiubo?	kee-oo-bvoh	How are things [Literally: What was there]? (Chile)
¿Qué pasó?	keh pah-soh	How are things [Literally: What happened]? (Mexico)

Trabajar: Working

Work and professions always are useful subjects for small talk. And for that discussion, you need **trabajar** *(trah-bvah-har)*, a regular verb that means "to work." Check out how these two people discuss their jobs:

✔ **Jane: ¿Dónde trabaja usted?** *(dohn-deh trah-bvah-Hah oos-tehd)* (Where do you work?)

✔ **Pedro: Trabajo en México; soy ingeniero.** *(trah-bvah-Hoh ehn meh-Hee-koh, sohy een-Heh-neeeh-roh)* (I work in Mexico [City]; I'm an engineer.)

✔ **Jane: ¿Para qué compañía trabaja?** *(pah-rah keh kohm-pah-nyeeah trah-bvah-Hah)* (What company do you work for?)

✔ **Pedro: Soy empresario independiente.** *(sohy ehm-preh-sah-reeoh een-deh-pehn-deeehn-teh)* (I'm an independent entrepreneur.)

✔ **Jane: ¿Cuántos empleados tiene?** *(kooahn-tohs ehm-pleh-ah-dohs teeeh-neh)* (How many employees do you have?)

✔ **Pedro: Tengo nueve empleados. ¿Y usted qué hace?** *(tehn-goh nooeh-bveh ehm-pleh-ah-dohs ee oos-tehd keh ah-seh)* (I have nine employees. What do you do?)

✔ **Jane: Soy dentista.** *(sohy dehn-tees-tah)* (I'm a dentist.)

✔ **Pedro: ¿Y dónde tiene su consultorio?** *(ee dohn-deh teeeh-neh soo kohn-sool-toh-reeoh)* (And where do you work?)

✔ **Jane: En Puebla.** *(ehn Poo-eh-bvlah)* (In Puebla.)

Entender: Understanding

Another useful verb for discussing your profession is the irregular verb **entender** *(ehn-tehn-dehr)* (to understand). Table 4-4 conjugates the present tense.

Table 4-4	Entender
Conjugation	*Pronunciation*
yo entiendo	yoh ehn-tee<u>ehn</u>-doh
tú entiendes	too ehn-tee<u>ehn</u>-dehs
él, ella, ello, uno, usted entiende	ehl, <u>eh</u>-yah, <u>eh</u>-yoh, <u>oo</u>-noh, <u>oos</u>-tehd enh-tee<u>ehn</u>-deh
nosotros entendemos	noh-<u>soh</u>-trohs ehn-tehn-<u>deh</u>-mohs
vosotros entendéis	bvoh-<u>soh</u>-trohs ehn-tehn-<u>deh</u>ees
ellos, ellas, ustedes entienden	<u>eh</u>-yohs, <u>eh</u>-yahs, oos-<u>teh</u>-dehs ehn-tee<u>ehn</u>-dehn

Here are some examples using the irregular verb **entender** that you may find useful:

- ✔ **Yo entiendo de enfermería.** *(yoh ehn-tee<u>ehn</u>-doh deh ehn-fehr-meh-<u>reeah</u>)* (I know about nursing.)

- ✔ **Francisca entiende de cocina.** *(frahn-<u>sees</u>-kah ehn-tee<u>ehn</u>-deh deh koh-<u>see</u>-nah)* (Francisca knows about cooking.)

- ✔ **Nosotros entendemos el problema.** *(noh-<u>soh</u>-trohs ehn-tehn-<u>deh</u>-mohs ehl proh-<u>bvleh</u>-mah)* (We understand the problem.)

- ✔ **Pedro no entiende.** *(<u>peh</u>-droh noh ehn-tee<u>ehn</u>-deh)* (Pedro doesn't understand.)

- ✔ **Ellos entienden lo que decimos.** *(<u>eh</u>-yohs ehn-tee<u>ehn</u>-dehn loh keh deh-<u>see</u>-mohs)* (They understand what we're saying.)

Vivir: Living

"Where do you live?" is as frequent a question as "where do you work?" when making small talk. So you need the verb **vivir** *(bvee-<u>bveer</u>)*, which is a regular verb and means "to live."

Say you're introduced to a family. They probably want to know where you live, and they may invite you to come again:

- ✔ **Family member: ¿Dónde vives?** *(dohn-deh bvee-bvehs)* (Where do you live?)

- ✔ **You: Busco un departamento pequeño.** *(bvoos-koh oon deh-pahr-tah-mehn-toh peh-keh-nyoh)* (I'm looking for a small apartment.)

- ✔ **Family member: A la vuelta, arriendan un departamentito.** *(ah lah bvooehl-tah ah-rreeehn-dahn oon deh-pahr-tah-mehn-tee-toh)* (Around the corner, they rent a little apartment.)

- ✔ **You: Bueno, voy a verlo.** *(bvooeh-noh bvoy ah bvehr-loh)* (Good, I'm going to see it.)

- ✔ **Family member: Te va a gustar.** *(teh bvah ah goos-tahr)* (You'll like it.)

- ✔ **You: Bueno, no quiero molestar más, tengo que irme.** *(bvooeh-noh noh keeeh-roh moh-lehs-tahr mahs tehn-goh keh eer-meh)* (Well, I don't want to bother you any more, I have to go.)

- ✔ **Family member: Aquí tienes tu casa.** *(ah-kee teeeh-nehs too kah-sah)* (This is your home.)

- ✔ **You: Muchas gracias.** *(moo-chahs grah-seeahs)* (Thanks a lot.)

- ✔ **Family member: Te invito a que vengas mañana a tomar el tecito con nosotros.** *(teh een-bvee-toh ah keh bvehn-gahs mah-nyah-nah ah toh-mahr el teh-see-toh kohn noh-soh-trohs)* (I invite you to come tomorrow for [a small] tea [with us].)

- ✔ **You: Lo haré con mucho gusto.** *(loh ah-reh kohn moo-choh goos-toh)* (I'd love to.)

Small-talk apologies

Sometimes, you may not understand what someone is saying. Or you bump into someone and want to excuse yourself. The following courtesy phrases can come in handy:

✔ **No entiendo.** *(noh ehn-tee__ehn__-doh)* (I don't understand.)

✔ **Lo lamento.** *(loh lah-__mehn__-toh)* (I regret it; I'm sorry.)

✔ **¡Perdone!** *(pehr-__doh__-neh)* (Excuse me!)

Say this when you bump into someone.

Grand Inquisitor: Questions

You may have heard about "The Five W's," which represent the questions that you need to ask to cover the basic information about a situation (who, what, where, when, and why). We've added three more questions to this group that you may find useful when you meet someone. Here are the key questions:

✔ **¿Quién?** *(kee__ehn__)* (Who?)

✔ **¿Qué?** *(keh)* (What?)

✔ **¿Dónde?** *(__dohn__-deh)* (Where?)

✔ **¿Cuándo?** *(koo__ahn__-doh)* (When?)

✔ **¿Por qué?** *(pohr keh)* (Why?)

✔ **¿Cómo?** *(__koh__-moh)* (How?)

✔ **¿Cuánto?** *(koo__ahn__-toh)* (How much?)

✔ **¿Cuál?** *(kooahl)* (Which?)

The following are examples of how to use these words:

✔ **¿Quién es él?** *(kee__ehn__ ehs ehl)* (Who is he?)

✔ **¿Qué hace usted?** *(keh __ah__-seh oos-__tehd__)* (What do you do?)

✔ **¿Dónde viven?** *(__dohn__-deh __bvee__-bvehn)* (Where do you live?)

✔ **¿Cuándo llegaron?** *(koo__ahn__-doh yeh-__gah__-rohn)* (When did you arrive?)

✔ **¿Por qué está aquí?** *(pohr keh ehs-__tah__ ah-__kee__)* (Why are you [formal] here? Why is he [she, it] here?)

✔ **¿Cómo es el camino?** *(koh-moh ehs ehl kah-mee-noh)* (What's the road like?)

✔ **¿Cuánto cuesta el cuarto?** *(kooahn-toh kooehs-tah ehl kooahr-toh)* (How much is the room?)

✔ **¿Cuál hotel es mejor?** *(kooahl oh-tehl ehs meh-Hohr)* (Which hotel is better?)

Notice that these question words have accent marks over some vowels. You may have seen these words elsewhere without the accents. The accents help distinguish how the word is being used. For example, you can use a word such as **quien** *(keeehn)*, which means "who," in two ways:

✔ In a sentence to refer to someone who did this or that. **Quien** has no accent when you use it this way.

✔ As a question — Who did it? — or as an exclamation — Who could have said that? To call your attention to the fact that you're using who as a question or an exclamation, it carries an accent, as in **¡quién!** or **¿quién?**

The accents don't change the way the words sound; you use them only in the written form of the language. When speaking, your inflection, or tone of voice, tells listeners how you're using the term in question.

Say that you meet someone on a plane and want to ask him where he's from. Here's how such a conversation may go:

✔ **Carlos: ¡Qué vuelo tan agradable!** *(keh bvooeh-loh tahn ah-grah-dah-bvleh)* (Such a pleasant flight!)

✔ **Juan: Sí, es un viaje tranquilo.** *(see ehs oon bveeah-Heh trahn-kee-loh)* (Yes, it's a peaceful trip.)

✔ **Carlos: ¿Viaja a menudo en avión?** *(bveeah-Hah ah meh-noo-doh ehn ah-bveeohn)* (Do you fly often?)

✔ **Juan: No, éste es mi primer vuelo.** *(noh, ehs-teh ehs mee pree-mehr bvooeh-loh)* (No, this is my first time flying.)

✔ **Carlos: ¿De dónde es usted?** *(deh dohn-deh ehs oos-tehd)* (Where are you from?)

✔ **Juan: Soy de Buenos Aires. ¿Y usted?** *(sohy deh bvooeh-nohs ahee-rehs. ee oos-tehd)* (I'm from Buenos Aires. And you?)

✔ **Carlos: Yo soy de Nueva York . . .** *(yoh sohy deh nooeh-bvah yohrk)* (I'm from New York . . .)

. . . **¿cómo es Buenos Aires?** *(koh-moh ehs bvooeh-nohs ahee-rehs)* (. . . what's Buenos Aires like?)

✔ **Juan: Es una ciudad grande y maravillosa.** *(ehs ooh-nah seeoo-dahd grahn-deh ee mah-rahbvee-yoh-sah)* (It's a large and wonderful city.)

A Rainy Day: Talking Weather

Weather is an obsession in temperate countries where conditions vary a great deal, but in warmer climates, weather is much less of an issue. Some cities in southern Mexico, for example, don't even do weather reports. But for those times when you do want to talk weather, here's how you can do it:

✔ **Rosa: ¿Cómo es el clima de Buenos Aires?** *(koh-moh ehs ehl klee-mah deh bvooeh-nohs ahee-rehs)* (What's Buenos Aires' climate like?)

✔ **Mario: Es muy agradable y templado.** *(ehs mooy ah-grah-dah-bvleh ee tehm-plah-doh)* (It's very pleasant and temperate.)

✔ **Rosa: ¿Llueve mucho?** *(yooeh-bveh moo-choh)* (Does it rain a lot?)

✔ **Mario: Sí, llueve todo el año, pero no mucho.** *(see, yooeh-bveh toh-doh ehl an-nyoh, peh-roh noh moo-choh)* (Yes, there's rain all year round, but not too much.)

✔ **Rosa: ¿Y también hay sol?** *(ee tahm-bvee<u>ehn</u> ahy sohl)* (And is it also sunny?)

✔ **Maria: Sí, hay sol casi todos los días.** *(see ahy sohl <u>kah</u>-see <u>toh</u>-dohs lohs <u>dee</u>ahs)* (Yes, it's sunny almost every day.)

✔ **Rosa: ¿No nieva nunca?** *(noh nee<u>eh</u>-bvah <u>noon</u>-kah)* (Does it ever snow?)

✔ **Maria: No, en Buenos Aires nunca nieva.** *(noh ehn bvoo<u>eh</u>-nohs ahee-rehs <u>noon</u>-kah nee<u>eh</u>-bvah)* (No, in Buenos Aires it never snows.)

How Is Your Family?

In Latin America, the family is the basic unit of society. People work, live, and function in consonance with their families. When visiting your Spanish-speaking neighbors, therefore, you can be more comfortable if you pay attention to the way that Latinos stress the importance of the family and of family relationships.

Table 4-5 gives basic names for family members.

Table 4-5	Family Members	
Spanish	*Pronunciation*	*Translation*
padre	<u>pah</u>-dreh	father
madre	<u>mah</u>-dreh	mother
hijo	<u>ee</u>-Hoh	son
hija	<u>ee</u>-Hah	daughter
hermano	ehr-<u>mah</u>-noh	brother
hermana	ehr-<u>mah</u>-nah	sister
yerno	<u>yehr</u>-noh	son-in-law
nuera	noo<u>eh</u>-rah	daughter-in-law

(continued)

Table 4-5 *(continued)*

Spanish	Pronunciation	Translation
nieto	nee_eh_-toh	grandson
nieta	nee_eh_-tah	granddaughter
cuñado	koo-_nyah_-doh	brother-in-law
cuñada	koo-_nyah_-dah	sister-in-law
primo	_pree_-moh	cousin [male]
prima	_pree_-mah	cousin [female]
padrino	pah-_dree_-noh	godfather
madrina	mah-_dree_-nah	godmother
tío	_tee_oh	uncle
tía	_tee_ah	aunt
abuelo	ah-bvoo_eh_-loh	grandfather
abuela	ah-bvoo_eh_-lah	grandmother

Chapter 5

Enjoying a Drink and a Snack (or Meal!)

• •

In This Chapter

▶ Getting a good meal vocabulary

▶ Asking simple questions at the restaurant

▶ Paying the check

• •

Getting the Table and Meal Basics

You may find these phrases useful when you plan a meal:

✔ **¡A poner la mesa!** *(ah poh-_nehr_ lah _meh_-sah)* (Set the table!)

✔ **Aquí están los platos y los vasos.** *(ah-_kee_ ehs-_tahn_ lohs _plah_-tohs ee lohs _bvah_-sohs)* (Here are the dishes and glasses.)

✔ **¿Qué cubiertos?** *(keh koo-bvee-_ehr_-tohs)* (What cutlery?)

✔ **Cuchara, cuchillo, tenedor, y cucharita.** *(koo-_chah_-rah koo-_chee_-yo teh-neh-_dohr_ ee koo-chah-_ree_-tah)* (Spoon, knife, fork, and coffee or demitasse spoon.)

✔ **Aquí están las servilletas.** *(ah-_kee_ ehs-_tahn_ lahs sehr-bvee-_yeh_-tahs)* (Here are the napkins.)

✔ **Más sal en el salero.** *(mahs sahl ehn ehl sah-_leh_-roh)* (More salt in the salt shaker.)

Here are some common terms connected with meals:

- **almuerzo** *(ahl-moo<u>ehr</u>-soh)* (lunch)
- **cena** *(<u>seh</u>-nah)* (supper)
- **comida** *(koh-<u>mee</u>-dah)* (dinner)
- **desayuno** *(deh-sah-<u>yoo</u>-noh)* (breakfast)
- **tengo sed** *(<u>tehn</u>-goh sehd)* (I'm thirsty)
- **tiene hambre** *(tee-<u>eh</u>-neh <u>ahm</u>-bvreh)* (he/she's hungry)

You may hear these phrases, or speak them yourself, when giving or receiving foods and beverages:

- **¡Buen provecho!** *(bvooehn proh-<u>bveh</u>-choh)* (Enjoy your meal!)

  The equivalent of the French *Bon appetit!*
- **¿Con qué está servido?** *(kohn keh ehs-<u>tah</u> sehr-<u>bvee</u>-doh)* (What does it come with?)
- **Está caliente.** *(ehs-<u>tah</u> kah-lee <u>ehn</u>-teh)* (It's hot [temperature].)
- **Está frío.** *(ehs-<u>tah</u> freeoh)* (It's cold.)
- **Está picante.** *(ehs-<u>tah</u> pee-<u>kahn</u>-teh)* (It's hot [spicy].)
- **Es sabroso.** *(ehs sah-<u>bvroh</u>-soh)* (It's tasty.)
- **Lamento, no tenemos . . .** *(lah-<u>mehn</u>-toh noh teh-<u>neh</u>-mohs)* (Sorry, we don't have any . . .)
- **¿Qué ingredientes tiene?** *(keh een-greh-dee <u>ehn</u>-tehs tee <u>eh</u>-neh)* (What are the ingredients?)
- **¿Qué más trae el plato?** *(keh mahs <u>trah</u>-eh ehl <u>plah</u>-toh)* (What else is in the dish?)

Three Verbs Used at the Table

When talking about drinking in Spanish, do it with two verbs. One is **tomar** *(toh-<u>mahr</u>)*; the other is **beber** *(bveh-<u>bvehr</u>)*. **Comer** *(koh-<u>mehr</u>)* is to eat.

To take and to drink: The verb tomar

Tomar (toh-*mahr*) means literally "to take" and often means exactly that. But when you say **tomar un refresco** (toh-*mahr* oon reh-*frehs*-koh), you're talking about drinking a soda, not literally taking one. And you know that's what you mean because you follow **tomar** with something you drink. So **tomar** is a verb with a certain imprecision.

Tomar is a regular verb of the **-ar** (ahr) group. The root of the verb is **tom-** (tohm), as you can see from Table 5-1.

Table 5-1	Tomar
Conjugation	*Pronunciation*
yo tomo	yoh toh-moh
tú tomas	too toh-mahs
él, ella, ello, uno, usted toma	ehl, eh-yah, eh-yoh, oo-noh, oos-tehd toh-mah
nosotros tomamos	noh-soh-trohs toh-mah-mohs
vosotros tomáis	bvoh-soh-trohs toh-mah-ees
ellos, ellas, ustedes toman	eh-yohs, eh-yahs, oos-teh-dehs toh-mahn

For drinking only: The verb beber

In the case of the verb **beber,** you can have no doubts: This verb applies to drinking only.

Beber (bveh-*bvehr*) is also a regular verb; it's from the **-er** (ehr) group. The root of the verb is: **beb-** (bvehbv), as you can see in Table 5-2.

Table 5-2	Beber
Conjugation	*Pronunciation*
yo bebo	yoh <u>bveh</u>-bvoh
tú bebes	too <u>bveh</u>-bvehs
él, ella, ello, uno, usted bebe	ehl, <u>eh</u>-yah, <u>eh</u>-yoh, <u>oo</u>-noh, oos-<u>tehd</u> <u>bveh</u>-bveh
nosotros bebemos	noh-<u>soh</u>-trohs bveh-<u>bveh</u>-mohs
vosotros bebéis	bvoh-<u>soh</u>-trohs bveh-<u>bvehees</u>
ellos, ellas, ustedes beben	<u>eh</u>-yohs, <u>eh</u>-yahs, oos-<u>teh</u>-dehs <u>bveh</u>-bvehn

For eating: The verb comer

Comer (*koh-<u>mehr</u>*) means "to eat." A regular verb from the **-er** (*ehr*) group, the root of this verb is **com-** (*kohm*), as Table 5-3 shows.

Table 5-3	Comer
Conjugation	*Pronunciation*
yo como	yoh <u>koh</u>-moh
tú comes	too <u>koh</u>-mehs
él, ella, ello, uno, usted come	ehl, <u>eh</u>-yah, <u>eh</u>-yoh, <u>oo</u>-noh, oos-<u>tehd</u> <u>koh</u>-meh
nosotros comemos	noh-<u>soh</u>-trohs koh-<u>meh</u>-mohs
vosotros coméis	bvoh-<u>soh</u>-trohs koh-<u>mehees</u>
ellos, ellas, ustedes comen	<u>eh</u>-yohs, <u>eh</u>-yahs, oos-<u>teh</u>-dehs <u>koh</u>-mehn

At the Restaurant

Going out to a restaurant and navigating the waitstaff and the menu is always fun, but it can also be a bit challenging.

The verb **querer** *(keh-rehr)* (to want or to wish) is very helpful at the restaurant. It's an irregular verb. Notice that the root **quer-** *(kehr)* is transformed into **quier-** *(kee-ehr)* with some pronouns. See Table 5-4.

Table 5-4	Querer
Conjugation	*Pronunciation*
querer	keh-rehr
yo quiero	yoh keeeh-roh
tú quieres	too keeeh-rehs
él, ella, ello, uno, usted quiere	ehl, eh-yah, eh-yoh, oo-noh, oos-tehd keeeh-reh
nosotros queremos	noh-soh-trohs keh-reh-mohs
vosotros queries	bvoh-soh-trohs keh-rehees
ellos, ellas, ustedes quieren	eh-yohs, eh-yahs, oos-teh-dehs keeeh-rehn

If you want to go to a nice restaurant, making a reservation always is wise. Here are some phrases that can help you do just that:

> ✔ **Quiero reservar una mesa para dos personas.** *(keeeh-roh reh-sehr-bvahr oo-nah meh-sah pah-rah dohs pehr-soh-nahs)* (I want to reserve a table for two people.)

> ✔ **¿Para qué hora será?** *(pah-rah keh oh-rah seh-rah)* (At what time?)

✔ **¿A nombre de quién?** *(ah nohm-bvreh deh keeehn)* (Under what name?)

✔ **Les esperamos.** *(lehs ehs-peh-rah-mohs)* (We'll wait for you.)

After you're at the restaurant, many people like to order an aperitif, or cocktail, before dinner. These phrases can help you when you're ordering something to drink:

✔ **¿Quieren algo para beber?** *(kee-eh-rehn ahl-goh pah-rah bveh-bvehr)* (Do you want anything to drink?)

✔ **¿Se sirven un agua de frutas?** *(seh seer-bvehn oon ah-gooah deh froo-tahs)* (Would you like a diluted fruit juice?)

✔ **Yo quiero un vaso de vino tinto.** *(yoh keeh-roh oon bvah-soh de bvee-noh teen-toh)* (I want a glass of red wine.)

✔ **Escoger un vino.** *(ehs-koh-Hehr oon bvee-noh)* (Choose a wine)

✔ **Un refresco.** *(oon reh-frehs-koh)* (a soda pop)

✔ **Tomar un trago.** *(toh-mahr oon trah-goh)* (Have a drink [alcoholic])

✔ **Un vaso de agua.** *(oon bvah-soh deh ah-gooah)* (A glass of water)

✔ **Un vaso de leche.** *(oon bvah-soh deh leh-cheh)* (A glass of milk)

✔ **Una cerveza.** *(oo-nah sehr-bveh-sah)* (I want a beer.)

And then, of course, you always need to know how to toast:

¡Salud! *(sah-lood)* (Cheers!)

Now for great eating! You can use the following phrases to order or understand what your waiter is asking you:

- ✔ **¿Están listos para ordenar?** *(ehs-tahn lees-tohs pah-rah ohr-deh-nahr)* (Are you ready to order?)

- ✔ **Yo quiero una ensalada mixta.** *(yoh kee-eh-roh oo-nah ehn-sah-lah-dah meeks-tah)* (I want a mixed [several vegetables] salad.)

- ✔ **¿Y de plato fuerte?** *(ee deh plah-toh foo-ehr-teh)* (And as the main course?)

- ✔ **¿Qué nos recomienda?** *(keh nohs reh-koh-mee-ehn-dah)* (What do you suggest?)

- ✔ **Tenemos dos platos especiales.** *(teh-neh-mohs dohs plah-tohs ehs-peh-seeah-lehs)* (We have two specials.)

- ✔ **¿Con qué está acompañado?** *(kohn keh ehs-tah ah-kohm-pah-nyah-doh)* (What does it come with?)

Inevitably, you want to wash your hands, freshen your makeup, or do something else that requires the use of a public bathroom. The following phrases can help you find the room you need.

- ✔ **¿Dónde están los baños?** *(dohn-deh ehs-tahn lohs bvah-nyohs)* (Where are the bathrooms?)

- ✔ **Los baños están al fondo, a la derecha.** *(lohs bvah-nyohs ehs-tahn ahl fohn-doh ah lah deh-reh-chah)* (The bathrooms are at the back, to the right.)

- ✔ **¿Es este el baño?** *(ehs ehs-teh ehl bvah-nyoh)* (Is this the bathroom?)

- ✔ **No, este no es el baño. Es ese.** *(noh ehs-teh noh ehs ehl bvah-nyoh ehs eh-se)* (No, this isn't the bathroom. It's that one.)

What's on the Menu?

A menu in a foreign language can be intimidating. This list identifies some of the most popular food and drink in Spanish:

✔ **Aguardiente** *(ah-gooahr-deeehn-teh)*, which translates as "fire water," is an aperitif and is made out of grapes. Other liquors include **tequila** *(teh-kee-lah)* and **mezcal** *(mehs-kahl)*, both made from cacti, or **pisco** *(pees-koh)*, a liquor also made out of grapes.

✔ **Agua** *(ah-gooah)* in Mexico can mean "water," which is its exact translation, but it can also be a beverage made with water, fruit, and sugar. All fruits, and some vegetables even, make refreshing aguas *(ah-gooahs)*.

✔ **Aguita** *(ah-goo-ee-tah)* (little water), can be an herb tea, served after a meal, in Chile.

✔ **Empanada** *(ehm-pah-nah-dah)* actually means "in bread." In Mexico, an **empanada** is a folded and stuffed corn tortilla. You can get **empanadas** made out of wheat dough, which is then folded and stuffed, in Argentina and Chile. Argentinians like theirs small. Chileans make theirs big. Either way, they're delicious!

✔ In Spain, a **tortilla** *(tohr-tee-yah)* is a potato, onion, and egg omelette that's often served at room temperature.

✔ In Mexico, **elote** *(eh-loh-teh)* is the name of tender corn, the kind you eat from the cob. The same thing in Argentina, Chile, Peru, and Bolivia is called **choclo** *(choh-kloh)*.

✔ Green beans in Mexico are called **ejotes** *(eh-Hoh-tehs)*. In South America, you find them under names like **porotos verdes** *(poh-roh-tohs bvehr-dehs)*, or **porotitos** *(poh-roh-tee-tohs)*. When the beans are dry, they're called **porotos** *(poh-roh-tohs)* in most of Spanish-speaking America, except in Mexico, where they are known as **frijoles** *(free-Hoh-lehs)*. Nowhere else can you see as great a variety of beans as in a Peruvian market. They come in enough colors and shapes and sizes to make your mouth water. You may want to try them all.

✔ In Chile, **filete** *(fee-leh-teh)* is the cut of beef called "sirloin" in the United States. In Argentina, the same cut is called **lomo** *(loh-moh)*.

✔ The basic Argentinean meal is **bife, con papas y ensalada** (*bvee-feh kohn pah-pahs ee ehn-sah-lah-dah*), which translates to "grilled steak, with potatoes and salad." On an Argentinean grill, you're likely to find a number of meats familiar to you, along with others that you probably never have eaten. Among the more exotic meats that fall into the "steak" category, you may find **chinchulín** (*cheen-choo-leen*), which is braided and grilled beef bowels. ¡**Delicioso!** Another delicacy is **molleja** (*moh-yeh-Hah*), which is the thyroid gland of a cow.

✔ In Mexico, **molleja** (*moh-yeh-Hah*) is chicken gizzard. And in Chile, the same chicken gizzard is **contre** (*kohn-treh*).

✔ The liver that you eat in Chile is called **pana** (*pah-nah);* in most other places in Latin America, liver is **hígado** (*ee-gah-doh*).

✔ In Spain, **jamón serrano** (*Ha-mohn seh-rran-oh*), salt-cured ham typical of the mountain regions, is a great delicacy.

Some fish and seafood favorites include

✔ **Loco** (*loh-koh*), a truly gigantic scallop, and **congrio** (*kohn-greeoh*), or conger eel, a type of fish.

✔ **Albacora** (*ahl-bvah-koh-rah*) (swordfish), **cangrejo** (*kahn-greh-Hoh*) (giant crab), **jaiba** (*Hahee-bvah*) (small crab), **langosta** (*lahn-gohs-tah*) (lobster); **langostino** (*lahn-gohs-tee-noh*) (prawn), **camarón** (*kah-mah-rohn*) (shrimp), and other delights to crowd your **sopa marinera** (*soh-pah mah-ree-neh-rah*) (fish soup).

✔ **Ceviche** (*seh-bvee-cheh*) made out of raw fish or raw seafood. **Ceviches** come in many varieties.

You also may want to order some of these specialties:

✔ Called **aguacate** (*ah-gooah-kah-teh*) in Mexico and **palta** (*pahl-tah*) in Argentina, Uruguay, and Chile, it's still the same "avocado."

✔ In the south of Mexico, when you say **pan** *(pahn)*, meaning "bread," people usually think of something that the baker made to taste sweet. In South America, **pan** is closer to what you eat in the States.

✔ **Torta** *(tohr-tah)* in Mexico is a sandwich in a bun (a "sandwich" is made with bread baked in a mold and sliced.) But most everywhere in Latin America, **torta** *(tohr-tah)* means "cake," and **sandwich** means "sandwich" (no matter how it's served).

✔ **Memelas** *(meh-meh-lahs)* in Mexico are tortillas that are pinched on the side to form a hollow, which is filled with pastes and delicacies.

✔ **Gazpacho** *(gahs-pah-choh)* is a chilled vegetable soup from Spain flavored with olive oil, garlic, and vinegar.

✔ In Spain, **paella** *(pah-eh-yah)* is a favorite dish made of seafood and saffron rice.

Some people say that the sauces make Latin American foods truly special. This statement is especially true of the sauces served in Mexico, which have an infinite variety of flavors and textures.

✔ **Mole** *(moh-leh)*, a word used in Mexico, means "sauce." These Mexican **moles** are served hot with meats and chicken:

✔ **Mole negro** *(moh-leh neh-groh)* (black mole) looks black — naturally! — and is made with all toasted ingredients: cocoa, chilies, almonds, onions, garlic, and bread. It can be very spicy or less so.

✔ **Mole colorado** *(moh-leh koh-loh-rah-doh)* (red mole) looks red and is made with chilies. It's spicy hot! The sauce is also called **coloradito** *(koh-loh-rah-dee-toh)*.

✔ **Mole amarillo** *(moh-leh ah-mah-ree-yoh)* (yellow mole) is orangy yellow. You make it with almonds and raisins, among other ingredients. Generally, it's only mildly spicy.

✔ **Mole verde** (*moh*-leh *bvehr*-deh) (green mole) is
made with green tomatoes, green chilies (hot
peppers), and coriander (cilantro) and looks
green. It can be very spicy or mildly hot.

Mexicans don't eat **moles** every day. They serve these
delicacies only on special occasions.

Mexicans also bring some cold sauces to the table to
add more spice to your food:

✔ **Pico de gallo** (*pee*-koh deh *gah*-yoh), which
translates as "rooster's beak," is made totally
with vegetables. It looks red, green, and white
because it's made with tomatoes, jalapeño peppers, coriander, and onions. Hot!

✔ **Guacamole** (gooah-kah-*moh*-leh) needs no translation. It's the dip made with avocado, **chili**
(*chee*-leh) (hot pepper), coriander (cilantro),
lemon, and salt. It's sometimes spicy hot.

✔ **Salsa verde** (*sahl*-sah *bvehr*-deh) green sauce
made with green tomatoes, chilies, and coriander. Hot!

✔ **Salsa roja** (*sahl*-sah *roh*-Hah) red sauce is made
with red tomatoes and chilies. Hot!

The Bill, Please

When you're finished eating and ready to go out danc-
ing for the evening, you're ready to pay your bill. Here
are some phrases that you may need to know:

✔ **Joven, ¿nos trae la cuenta por favor?** (*Hoh*-
bveh nohs *trah*-eh lah koo*ehn*-tah pohr fah-*bvohr*)
(Waiter, will you bring us the check please?)

✔ **¿Aceptan tarjetas de crédito?** (ah-*sehp*-tahn
tahr-*Heh*-tahs deh *kreh*-dee-toh) (Do you accept
credit cards?)

✔ **¿Dejamos propina?** (deh-*Hah*-mohs proh-*pee*-
nah) (Did we leave a tip?)

Chapter 6

Shop 'Til You Drop

• •

In This Chapter

▶ Finding the right stores and the right clothes

▶ Visiting the food markets

▶ Bartering for your finds

▶ Knowing the good from the best (language-wise)

• •

*E*ven experienced shoppers can enjoy new ways to shop and new stores to shop at. Whether shopping is fun or hard work for you, in this chapter, we explain how to go about it Latin style!

Heading Out on the Town

No matter what type of shopping you're planning to do, you always want to find out whether the store is open. Here's how to ask for that information:

> ✔ **¿A qué hora abren?** *(ah keh oh-rah ah-bvrehn)* (At what time do you [formal] open?)

> ✔ **¿A qué hora cierran?** *(ah keh oh-rah seeeh-rrahn)* (At what time do you [formal] close?)

Browsing around

You're out shopping for clothes, but you're just browsing for now. Here's what the clerk may ask and what you can answer:

✔ **¿Busca algo en especial?** *(bvoos-kah ahl-goh ehn ehs-peh-seeahl)* (Looking for something special?)

✔ **Quiero mirar no más.** *(keeeh-roh mee-rahr noh mahs)* (I just want to look.)

✔ **Me llama cuando me necesita.** *(meh yah-mah kooahn-doh meh neh-seh-see-tah)* (Call me when you need me.)

✔ **Sí, le voy a llamar, gracias.** *(see leh bvohy ah yah-mahr grah-seeahs)* (Yes, I'll call you, thank you.)

Getting around the store

Now you're ready for some help:

✔ **¿Dónde están los vestidos de señora?** *(dohn-deh ehs-tahn lohs bvehs-tee-dohs deh seh-nyoh-rah)* (Where are the ladies' clothes?)

✔ **¿Dónde está la ropa de hombre?** *(dohn-deh ehs-tah lah roh-pah deh ohm-bvreh)* (Where are the men's clothes?)

✔ **¿Dónde encuentro artículos de tocador?** *(dohn-deh ehn-kooehn-troh ahr-tee-koo-lohs deh toh-kah-dohr)* (Where do I find toiletries?)

✔ **Busco la sección de ropa blanca.** *(bvoos-koh lah sehk-seeohn deh roh-pah bvlahn-kah)* (I'm looking for sheets and towels.)

✔ **¿Venden electrodomésticos?** *(bvehn-dehn eehl-ehk-troh-doh-mehs-tee-kohs)* (Do you sell appliances?)

The salesperson may give you any of these answers:

✔ **En el cuarto piso.** *(ehn ehl kooahr-toh pee-soh)* (On the fourth floor.)

✔ **Al fondo, a la izquierda.** *(ahl fohn-doh ah lah ees-keeehr-dah)* (At the back, to the left.)

✔ **Un piso más arriba.** *(oon pee-soh mahs ah-rree-bvah)* (One floor up.)

✔ **En el último piso.** *(ehn ehl ool-tee-moh pee-soh)* (On the top floor.)

Here are a few more phrases to help you out:

- ✔ **¿Dónde está la entrada?** *(dohn-deh ehs-tah lah ehn-trah-dah)* (Where's the entrance?)

- ✔ **¿Dónde está la salida?** *(dohn-deh ehs-tah lah sah-lee-dah)* (Where's the exit?)

- ✔ **empuje** *(ehm-poo-Heh)* (push)

- ✔ **tire** *(tee-reh)* (pull)

- ✔ **jale** *(Hah-leh)* (pull [Mexico])

- ✔ **el ascensor** *(ehl ah-sehn-sohr)* (the elevator)

- ✔ **la escalera mecánica** *(lah ehs-kah-leh-rah meh-kah-nee-kah)* (the escalator)

- ✔ **el vendedor** *(ehl bvehn-deh-dohr)* or **la vendedora** *(lah bvehn-deh-doh-rah)* (the salesperson [male and female])

- ✔ **la caja** *(lah kah-Hah)* (the check out stand)

Requesting color and size

When you're ready to get more specific, ask for the color and size that you want:

- ✔ **¿Me ayuda por favor?** *(meh ah-yoo-dah porh fah-bvohr)* (Will you help me, please?)

- ✔ **Busco una falda, con bolsillos.** *(bvoos-koh oo-nah fahl-dah kohn bvohl-see-yohs)* (I'm looking for a skirt, with pockets.)

- ✔ **¿Qué talla tiene?** *(keh tah-yah teeeh-neh)* (What's your size?)

- ✔ **Talla doce americana.** *(tah-yah doh-seh ah-meh-ree-kah-nah)* (Size twelve, American.)

- ✔ **¿Me permite medirla, para estar seguras?** *(meh pehr-mee-teh meh-deer-lah pah-rah ehs-tahr seh-goo-rahs)* (May I take your size so we can know for sure?)

- ✔ **Ah, su talla es treinta y ocho.** *(ah soo tah-yah ehs treheen-tah ee oh-choh)* (Ah, your size is thirty-eight.)

✔ **¿Qué color busca?** *(keh koh-lohr bvoos-kah)* (What color are you looking for?)

✔ **Rojo.** *(roh-Hoh)* (Red.)

✔ **¿La quiere con flores?** *(lah keeeh-reh kohn floh-rehs)* (Do you want it with flowers?)

✔ **No, lisa, por favor.** *(noh lee-sah pohr fah-bvohr)* (No, plain, please.)

Words to Know

ayudar	ah-yoo-dahr	to help
más	mahs	more
menos	meh-nohs	less
la falda	lah fahl-dah	the skirt
el bolsillo	ehl bvohl-see-yoh	the pocket
medir	meh-deer	to measure
la talla	lah tah-yah	the size
liso	lee-soh	plain; flat

Table 6-1 gives you all the colors to choose from.

Table 6-1	Selecting Your Colors	
Color	*Pronunciation*	*Translation*
blanco	bvlahn-koh	white
negro	neh-groh	black
gris	grees	grey
rojo	roh-Hoh	red

Color	Pronunciation	Translation
azul	ah-*sool*	blue
verde	*bvehr*-deh	green
morado	moh-*rah*-doh	purple
violeta	bveeoh-*leh*-tah	violet, purple
café	kah-*feh*	brown
marrón	mah-*rrohn*	brown (Argentina)
amarillo	ah-mah-*ree*-yoh	yellow
naranja	nah-*rahn*-Hah	orange
rosado	roh-*sah*-doh	pink
celeste	seh-*lehs*-teh	sky blue
claro	*klah*-roh	light
oscuro	ohs-*koo*-roh	dark

Getting the right fit

To get the right fit, you may need to try the clothing on:

- ✔ **¿Puedo probarme este pantalón?** *(pooeh-doh proh-bvahr-meh ehs-teh pahn-tah-lohn)* (May I try on these trousers?)

- ✔ **Cómo no, por aquí.** *(koh-moh no pohr ah-kee)* (Of course, this way.)

- ✔ **Pase al probador, por favor.** *(pah-seh ahl proh-bvah-dohr pohr fah-bvohr)* (Please go into the fitting room.)

- ✔ **¿Le quedó bien?** *(leh keh-doh bveeehn)* (Did it fit?)

- ✔ **Me queda grande.** *(meh keh-dah grahn-deh)* (They are too big. [Literally: It fits me large.])

✔ **Le busco otro.** *(leh bvoos-koh oh-troh)* (I'll find you another.)

✔ **Éste aprieta aquí.** *(ehs-teh ah-preeeh-tah ah-kee)* (This one is tight here.)

✔ **¿Puede traer una de talla más grande?** *(pooeh-deh trah-ehr oo-nah tah-yah mahs grahn-deh)* (Can you bring a larger size?)

✔ **Queda muy bien.** *(keh-dah mooy bveeehn)* (It fits very well.)

Words to Know

el probador	ehl proh-bvah-dohr	the fitting room
apretado	ah-preh-tah-doh	tight
suelto	sooehl-toh	loose
grande	grahn-deh	large
pequeño	peh-keh-nyoh	small
los pantalones	lohs pahn-tah-loh-nehs	the trousers
queda grande	keh-dah grahn-deh	the fit is big
queda bien	keh-dah bveeehn	the fit is right
probar	proh-bvahr	to try

Using the shopping verb: Comprar

Comprar *(kohm-prahr)* means "to shop," and **ir de compras** *(eer deh kohm-prahs)* means "to go shopping." **Comprar** is a regular verb of the **-ar** *(ahr)* group (check out Chapter 2 for the conjugation). These phrases, based on **ir de compras** _(eer deh kohm-prahs)_ (to go shopping), can help you at the market:

✔ **Fue de compras.** _(fooeh deh kohm-prahs)_ (She or he is out shopping.)

✔ **¡Voy de compras!** _(bvoy deh kohm-prahs)_ (I'm going shopping!)

✔ **¡Vamos de compras al mercado!** _(bvah-mohs deh kohm-prahs ahl-mehr-kah-do)_ (Let's go shopping at the market!)

Wearing and taking: The verb llevar

Whether you're wearing, tearing, or shopping, this is a great verb to have around.

In Spanish, "to wear," "to take with you," "to keep track of," and "to keep count of" are all the same verb — **llevar** _(yeh-bvahr)_. Good news! This is a regular verb of the group ending in **-ar**.

Another way to say to wear is **vestir** _(bvehs-teer)_ (to dress), which comes from **vestido** _(bves-tee-doh)_ (dress).

Here' are some helpful **llevar** phrases:

✔ **Me llevo esta camisa.** _(meh yeh-bvoh ehs-tah kah-mee-sah)_ (I'll take this shirt.)

✔ **El vestido que llevas es bellísimo.** _(ehl bvehs-tee-doh keh yeh-bvahs ehs bveh-yee-see-moh)_ (The dress you have on is very beautiful.)

✔ **Él lleva cuenta de cuántos vestidos compraste.** _(ehl yeh-bvah kooehn-tah deh kooahn-tohs bvehs-tee-dohs kohm-prahs-teh)_ (He keeps track of the number of dresses you buy.)

✔ **La llevo.** _(lah yeh-bvoh)_ (I'll take it.)

Shopping the Traditional Market

In this section, you visit markets that may be open or under a roof but are more informal than supermarkets. Also, in these markets, vendors are salespeople, not just cashiers, and they may approach you to sell you goods that you may or may not want. When you don't want something, you can simply say one of the following:

✔ **Ahora no, gracias.** *(ah-oh-rah noh grah-seeahs)* (Not now, thank you.)

✔ **Ya tengo, gracias.** *(yah tehn-goh grah-seeahs)* (I already have some, thanks.)

✔ **No me interesa, gracias.** *(no meh een-teh-reh-sah grah-seeahs)* (It doesn't interest me, thank you.)

✔ **Más tarde, gracias.** *(mahs tahr-deh grah-seeahs)* (Later, thank you.)

✔ **No me gusta, gracias.** *(noh meh goos-tah grah-seeahs)* (I don't like it, thanks.)

✔ **No me moleste, ¡por favor!** *(noh meh moh-lehs-teh pohr fah-bvohr)* (Don't bother me, please!)

Shopping for food

Table 6-2 lists the names of fruits you find at the market.

Table 6-2	Fruit	
Fruit	*Pronunciation*	*Translation*
la cereza	lah seh-reh-sah	the cherry
la ciruela	lah see-ro-eh-lah	the plum
el durazno	ehl doo-rahs-noh	the peach
el melocotón	ehl meh-loh-koh-tohn	the peach [in Spain]

Fruit	Pronunciation	Translation
la fresa	la <u>freh</u>-sah	the strawberry [Mexico, Central America, and Spain]
la frutilla	lah froo-<u>tee</u>-yah	the strawberry [from Colombia to the South Pole]
la guayaba	lah gooah-<u>yah</u>-bvah	the guava
el higo	ehl <u>ee</u>-goh	the fig
la lima	lah <u>lee</u>-mah	the lime
el limón	ehl lee-<u>mohn</u>	the lemon
el mango	ehl <u>mahn</u>-goh	the mango
la manzana	lah mahn-<u>sah</u>-nah	the apple
el melón	ehl meh-<u>lohn</u>	the melon
la mora	lah <u>moh</u>-rah	the blackberry
la naranja	lah nah-<u>rahn</u>-Hah	the orange
la papaya	lah pah-<u>pah</u>-yah	the papaya
la pera	lah <u>peh</u>-rah	the pear
el plátano	ehl <u>plah</u>-tah-noh	the banana
el pomelo	ehl poh-<u>meh</u>-loh	the grapefruit [in Mexico]
la sandía	lah sahn-<u>deea</u>h	the watermelon
la toronja	lah toh-<u>rohn</u>-Ha	the grapefruit [in Mexico]
la tuna	lah <u>too</u>-nah	the prickly pear
la uva	lah <u>oo</u>-bvah	the grape

Fresh vegetables are always good. You can easily find the ones listed in Table 6-3.

Table 6-3	Vegetables	
Vegetable	*Pronunciation*	*Translation*
las acelgas	lahs ah-<u>sehl</u>-gahs	the swiss chard
el aguacate	ehl ah-gooah-<u>kah</u>-teh	the avocado
el ají	el <u>ah</u>-Hee	the hot pepper [South America]
el ajo	ehl <u>ah</u>-Hoh	the garlic
el brócoli	ehl <u>bvroh</u>-koh-lee	the broccoli
la calabacita	lah kah-lah-bvah-<u>see</u>-tah	the zucchini [Mexico]
la calabaza	lah kah-lah-<u>bvah</u>-sah	the pumpkin [Central America and Mexico]
las cebollas	lahs seh-<u>bvoh</u>-yahs	the onions
el chile	ehl <u>chee</u>-leh	the hot pepper [Mexico and Guatemala]
el chile morrón	ehl <u>chee</u>-leh moh-<u>rrohn</u>	the sweet pepper [Mexico]
la col	lah kohl	the cabbage [Mexico]
la coliflor	lah koh-lee-<u>flohr</u>	the cauliflower
la espinaca	lah ehs-pee-<u>nah</u>-kah	the spinach
la lechuga	lah leh-<u>choo</u>-gah	the lettuce
las papas	lahs <u>pah</u>-pahs	the potatoes; patatas pah-<u>tah</u>-tahs in Spain
la palta	lah <u>pahl</u>-tah	the avocado [South America]
el pimentón	ehl pee-mehn-<u>tohn</u>	the sweet pepper [Argentina, Chile, and Uruguay]

Vegetable	Pronunciation	Translation
el repollo	ehl reh-<u>poh</u>-yoh	the cabbage [Argentina and Chile]
la zanahoria	lah sah-nah-<u>oh</u>-reeah	the carrot
el zapallito	ehl sah-pah-<u>yee</u>-toh	zucchini [Uruguay and Argentina]
el zapallo	ehl sah-<u>pah</u>-yoh	the pumpkin [South America]

Here are some of the fish and seafood you may be choosing among in the marketplace:

- ✔ **el camarón** *(kah-mah-<u>rohn</u>)* (shrimp); **gambas** *(<u>gahm</u>-bahs)* in Spain
- ✔ **el congrio** *(ehl <u>kohn</u>-greeoh)* (conger eel [coasts of Chile and Peru])
- ✔ **el huachinango** *(ehl ooah-chee-<u>nahn</u>-goh)* (red snapper)
- ✔ **el langostino** *(ehl lahn-gohs-<u>tee</u>-noh)* (prawn)
- ✔ **el marisco** *(ehl mah-<u>rees</u>-koh)* (seafood)
- ✔ **el pescado** *(ehl pehs-<u>kah</u>-doh)* (fish)
- ✔ **la trucha** *(lah <u>troo</u>-chah)* (trout)

You may hear (or need to say) these phrases when selecting what fish to buy:

- ✔ **Quiero la trucha.** *(<u>keeeh</u>-roh lah <u>troo</u>-chah)* (I want the trout.)
- ✔ **Lo quiero fileteado, sin espinas.** *(loh <u>keeeh</u>-roh fee-leh-teh-<u>ah</u>-doh seen ehs-<u>pee</u>-nahs)* (I want it filleted, boneless.)
- ✔ **¿Se lleva la cabeza para la sopa?** *(seh <u>yeh</u>-bvah lah kah-<u>bveh</u>-sah <u>pah</u>-rah lah <u>soh</u>-pah)* (Will you take the head for the soup?)

✔ **Sí, aparte, por favor.** *(see ah-_pahr_-teh pohr fah-_bvohr_)* (Yes, separately, please.)

Scoping out special items

You should know these phrases when shopping at a specialized store or gallery:

✔ **Busco grabados de Rufino Tamayo.** *(_bvoos_-koh grah-_bvah_-dohs deh roo-_fee_-noh tah-_mah_-yoh)* (I'm looking for etchings by Rufino Tamayo.)

✔ **¿Tiene broches de plata?** *(teee_eh_-neh _bvroh_-chehs deh _plah_-tah)* (Do you have silver brooches?)

✔ **¿Cuánto cuesta el collar que tiene en la ventana?** *(koo_ahn_-toh koo_ehs_-tah ehl koh-_yahr_ keh teee_eh_-neh ehn la bvehn-_tah_-nah)* (How much is the necklace you have in the window?)

✔ **¿Y la pintura?** *(ee lah peen-_too_-rah)* (And the painting?)

✔ **¿Vende perlas del sur de Chile?** *(_bvehn_-deh _pehr_-lahs dehl soor deh _chee_-leh)* (Do you sell pearls from the south of Chile?)

✔ **¿De quién es la escultura en la vitrina?** *(deh keee_ehn_ ehs lah ehs-kool-_too_-rah ehn lah bvee-_tree_-nah)* (By whom is the sculpture in the display case?)

✔ **¿Lo embalamos y mandamos a su domicilio?** *(loh ehm-bvah-_lah_-mohs ee mahn-_dah_-mohs a soo doh-mee-_see_-leeoh)* (Shall we pack it and send it to your address?)

✔ **¿Dónde venden objetos de cobre?** *(_dohn_-deh _bvehn_-dehn ohbv-_Heh_-tohs deh _koh_-bvreh)* (Where do they sell copper objects?)

✔ **Busco objetos de vidrio.** *(_bvoos_-koh ohbv-_Heh_-tohs deh _bvee_-dreeoh)* (I'm looking for glass objects.)

✔ **Allí hay cerámica hecha a mano.** *(ah-_kee_ ahy seh-_rah_-mee-kah _eh_-chah ah _mah_-noh)* (There are some hand-made ceramics.)

✔ **Estas ollas de barro sirven para cocinar.** (*ehs-tahs <u>oh</u>-yahs deh <u>bvah</u>-rroh <u>seer</u>-bvehn <u>pah</u>-rah koh-see-<u>nahr</u>*) (These clay pots are suitable for cooking.)

Words to Know

la alfombra	lah ahl-<u>fohm</u>-bvrah	rug
la bombilla	lah bvohm-<u>bvee</u>-yah	a tube, with filter, used to drink mate (<u>mah</u>-teh)
la olla	lah <u>oh</u>-yah	the pot
el barro	ehl <u>bvah</u>-rroh	the clay
rebajar	reh-bvah-<u>Hahr</u>	to bring the price down
el dibujo	ehl dee-<u>bvoo</u>-Hoh	the drawing; the pattern
el cobre	ehl <u>koh</u>-bvreh	the copper
el vidrio	ehl <u>bvee</u>-dreeoh	the glass
soplar	soh-<u>plahr</u>	to blow
hecho a mano	<u>eh</u>-choh ah <u>mah</u>-noh	handmade
la cerámica	lah seh-<u>rah</u>-mee-kah	the ceramic

Visiting the Supermarket

Following are some words and phrases that can help you at the supermarket:

- ✔ **el arroz** *(ehl ah-rrohs)* (the rice)
- ✔ **el atún** *(ehl ah-toon)* (the tuna)
- ✔ **el fideo** *(ehl fee-deh-oh)* (the pasta)
- ✔ **los cereales** *(lohs seh-reh-ah-lehs)* (the cereals)
- ✔ **las galletas** *(lahs gah-yeh-tahs)* (the cookies or crackers)
- ✔ **la leche** *(lah leh-cheh)* (the milk)
- ✔ **pagar** *(pah-gahr)* (to pay)
- ✔ **el pasillo** *(ehl pah-see-yoh)* (the aisle)
- ✔ **las sardinas** *(lahs sahr-dee-nahs)* (the sardines)
- ✔ **el vino** *(ehl bvee-noh)* (the wine)
- ✔ **el vuelto** *(ehl bvooehl-toh)* (change [as in money back]); **la vuelta** *(lah bvoo-ehl-tah)* in Spain
- ✔ **las ollas** *(lahs oh-yas)* (pots)
- ✔ **el tercer pasillo** *(ehl tehr-sehr pah-see-yoh)* (the third aisle)
- ✔ **Al fondo** *(ahl fohn-doh)* (at the back)
- ✔ **Gracias, aquí está su vuelto.** *(grah-seeahs ah-kee ehs-tah soo bvooehl-toh)* (Thanks, here's your change.)

Bartering for Your Goods

If you shop in traditional markets, you should get there early. Many merchants feel that they must make a first sale to kick off their day. If you find yourself in such a situation, you may notice that the merchant doesn't want you to leave without buying something and is therefore more willing to reduce the price to make a sale, and you can end up with a bargain.

The following phrases help you when you need to haggle in the market place:

- ✔ **¿Cuánto cuesta?** *(koo<u>ahn</u>-toh koo<u>ehs</u>-tah)* (How much is it?)

- ✔ **¿Cuánto vale?** *(koo<u>ahn</u>-toh <u>bvah</u>-leh)* (How much is it worth?)

- ✔ **¿A cuánto?** *(ah koo<u>ahn</u>-toh)* (How much?)

- ✔ **Es barato.** *(ehs bvah-<u>rah</u>-toh)* (It's cheap/inexpensive.)

- ✔ **Es caro.** *(ehs <u>kah</u>-roh)* (It's expensive.)

Use these phrases to provide emphasis. You don't need to use these all the time, especially the second and third ones, but they're fun to use and help you express a certain level of emotion:

- ✔ **¡Una ganga!** *(<u>oo</u>-nah <u>gahn</u>-gah)* (A bargain!)

- ✔ **¡Un robo!** *(oon <u>roh</u>-bvoh)* (A burglary!)

- ✔ **¡Un asalto!** *(oon ah-<u>sahl</u>-toh)* (A holdup!)

Are you ready to barter? Use these phrases to try it out:

- ✔ **Este tapete, ¿cuánto cuesta?** *(<u>ehs</u>-teh tah-<u>peh</u>-teh koo<u>ahn</u>-toh koo<u>ehs</u>-tah)* (How much is this rug?)

- ✔ **Quinientos pesos.** *(kee-nee<u>ehn</u>-tohs <u>peh</u>-sohs)* (Five hundred pesos.)

- ✔ **¿Tiene otros más baratos?** *(tee<u>eh</u>-neh <u>oh</u>-trohs mahs bvah-<u>rah</u>-tohs)* (Do you have cheaper ones?)

- ✔ **Tengo este, más pequeño.** *(<u>tehn</u>-goh <u>ehs</u>-teh mahs peh-<u>keh</u>-nyoh)* (I have this smaller one.)

- ✔ **No me gusta el dibujo.** *(noh meh <u>goos</u>-tah ehl dee-<u>bvoo</u>-Hoh)* (I don't like the pattern.)

- ✔ **Este en blanco y negro, a trescientos.** *(<u>ehs</u>-teh ehn <u>bvlahn</u>-koh ee <u>neh</u>-groh ah trehs-see<u>ehn</u>-tohs)* (This black and white one, for three hundred.)

- ✔ **Me gusta. ¿A doscientos?** *(meh <u>goos</u>-tah ah dohs-see<u>ehn</u>-tohs)* (I like it. Two hundred?)

✔ **No puedo. Doscientos cincuenta. Último precio.**
(noh pooeh-doh dohs-seeehn-tohs seen-kooehn-tah ool-tee-moh preh-seeoh) (I can't. Two hundred and fifty. Last price.)

✔ **Bueno, me lo llevo.** *(bvooeh-noh meh loh yeh-bvoh)* (Good. I'll take it.)

Getting the Right Quantity

A **kilo** *(kee-loh)* is a bit more than two pounds. **Kilo** actually comes from the word *kilogram,* which means one thousand grams. One gram is **un gramo** *(oon grah-moh).* One gram is a very small amount — roughly equivalent to the weight of the water filling a thimble. A **litro** *(lee-troh)* or "liter," is four cups, like a quart. Here's a list of other quantities:

✔ **una docena** *(oo-nah doh-seh-nah)* (a dozen)

✔ **media docena** *(meh-deeah doh-seh-nah)* (a half dozen)

✔ **una cincuentena** *(oo-nah seen-kooehn-teh-nah)* (fifty; 50)

✔ **una centena** *(oo-nah sehn-teh-nah)* (one hundred; 100)

✔ **un millar** *(oon mee-yahr)* (one thousand; 1,000)

Comparing Better or Best

When you compare one thing to another, you talk in comparatives and superlatives. In Spanish, most of the time you use the word **más** *(mahs)* (more) for comparisons and **el más** *(ehl mahs),* which literally means "the most," for superlatives. An example is the word **grande** *(grahn-deh),* which means "large" in English. **Más grande** *(mahs grahn-deh)* means "larger," and **el más grande** *(ehl mahs grahn-deh)* means "the largest."

In English, you usually change the word's ending; in Spanish, you just add **más** or **el más.** English has a similar system of adding comparatives and superlatives for longer words, such as *expensive,* where the comparative adds "more" before expensive, and the superlative adds "most."

Here are some examples of Spanish comparatives and superlatives:

✔ **grande** *(grahn-deh)* (big; large)

  más grande *(mahs grahn-deh)* (bigger; larger)

  el más grande *(ehl mahs grahn-deh)* (biggest; largest)

✔ **pequeño** *(peh-keh-nyoh)* (small)

  más pequeño *(mahs peh-keh-nyoh)* (smaller)

  el más pequeño *(ehl mahs peh-keh-nyoh)* (smallest)

✔ **chico** *(chee-koh)* (small; short; young)

  más chico *(mahs chee-koh)* (smaller; shorter; younger)

  el más chico *(ehl mahs chee-koh)* (smallest; shortest, youngest)

✔ **apretado** *(ah-preh-tah-doh)* (tight)

  más apretado *(mahs ah-preh-tah-doh)* (tighter)

  el más apretado *(ehl mahs ah-preh-tah-doh)* (tightest)

✔ **suelto** *(sooehl-toh)* (loose)

  más suelto *(mahs sooehl-toh)* (looser)

  el más suelto *(ehl mahs sooehl-toh)* (loosest)

✔ **caro** *(kah-roh)* (expensive)

  más caro *(mahs kah-roh)* (more expensive)

  el más caro *(ehl mahs kah-roh)* (most expensive)

✔ **barato** *(bvah-rah-toh)* (cheap)

más barato *(mahs bvah-rah-toh)* (cheaper)

el más barato *(ehl mahs bvah-rah-toh)* (cheapest)

Just as in English, a few exceptions exist, in which the comparative form doesn't need the word **más,** such as

✔ **bueno** *(bvooeh-noh)* (good)

mejor *(meh-Hohr)* (better)

el mejor *(ehl meh-Hohr)* (best)

✔ **malo** *(mah-loh)* (bad)

peor *(peh-ohr)* (worse)

el peor *(ehl peh-ohr)* (worst)

Notice that the English meanings also are exceptions to the English rules for forming comparatives and superlatives.

But maybe "the best" is good enough for you. Spanish speakers love to exaggerate. So in Spanish, you can't only compare things, you also have a way to express an exaggerated state of things.

To say that something is exaggeratedly this or that, you add **-ísimo** *(ee-see-moh)* or **-ísima** *(ee-see-mah)* to an adjective or an adverb. For example, to say that something good, **bueno** *(bvooeh-noh),* is exaggeratedly so, you say **buenísimo** *(bvooeh-nee-see-moh)* (exceptionally good).

Chapter 7

Making Leisure a Top Priority

. . . .

In This Chapter

▶ Enjoying city night life

▶ Getting outdoors

▶ Playing sports

. . . .

*Y*ou have no chance of getting bored in Latin American circles. Be it music, movies, theater, or dance — you name it — you have much to see and experience.

Latinos love culture, and they rejoice in turning their cultural activities into social events — gathering with old friends and new arrivals for movies, concerts, the opera, or whatever. They also love their sports.

Having a Good Time

The pleasure that people take in cultural expression is universal. Everyone loves a good show. Here are some phrases Spanish speakers use to express their culture:

✔ **¡Bailar y cantar!** *(bahee-lahr ee kahn-tahr)* (Dance and sing!)

✔ **¡Ésta es para ti!** *(ehs-tah ehs pah-rah tee!)* (This one is for you! [from a Cuban song])

When, where, and how long are party questions that need answers:

- ✔ **¿A qué hora comienza la fiesta?** *(ah keh oh-rah koh-meeehn-sah la feeehs-tah)* (What time does the party start?)

- ✔ **¿No será muy tarde?** *(noh seh-rah mooy tahr-deh)* (Won't it be too late?)

- ✔ **¿A qué hora acaba la fiesta?** *(ah keh oh-rah ah-kah-bvah lah feeehs-tah)* (What time will the party end?)

- ✔ **¿Hasta qué hora?** *(ahs-tah keh oh-rah)* (Until what time?)

- ✔ **Dicen que dura hasta las dos de la mañana.** *(dee-sehn keh doo-rah ahs-tah lahs dohs deh lah mah-nyah-nah)* (They say it lasts until two in the morning.)

- ✔ **¿Dónde va a ser la fiesta?** *(dohn-deh bvah ah sehr lah feeehs-tah)* (Where's the party going to be?)

- ✔ **En el Mesón del Angel.** *(ehn ehl meh-sohn dehl ahn-Hehl)* (At the Angel Meson.)

Using the inviting verb invitar

You need to be familiar with the verb "to invite," which in Spanish is **invitar** *(een-bvee-tahr)*, in case you're asked to a party by a Spanish-speaking acquaintance. Good news! **Invitar** is a regular verb of the **-ar** variety (see Chapter 2 for the conjugation). Use the following phrases to help you give and receive invitations.

- ✔ **Te invito al teatro.** *(teh een-bvee-toh ahl teh-ah-troh)* (I invite you to the theater.)

- ✔ **Nos invitan al baile.** *(nohs een-bvee-tahn ahl bvaee-leh)* (We are invited to the dance.)

- ✔ **Ellos invitan a todos a la fiesta.** *(eh-yohs een-bvee-tahn ah toh-dohs la feeehs-tah)* (They invite everybody to the fiesta.)

✔ **Tenemos que invitarlos a la casa.** *(teh-neh-mohs keh een-bvee-tahr-lohs ah la kah-sah)* (We have to invite them to our place.)

✔ **Voy a invitarlos al concierto.** *(bvohy ah een-bvee-tahr-lohs ahl kohn-seeehr-toh)* (I'm going to invite them to the concert.)

Notice the use of **al** *(ahl)* (to the) in phrases like **al teatro** and **al baile. Teatro** and **baile** are masculine words that would normally take the article **el.** But **a el,** formed when you add the preposition **a** *(ah)* (to) to the mix, sounds unpleasant to the Spanish ear. So Spanish joins the two words into **al.** That sounds much smoother, don't you think?

Using the dancing verb bailar

Bailar *(bvahee-lahr)* (to dance) is a regularly beautiful verb, great to swing along to. The root of this verb is **bail-** *(bvahee-)*.

These phrases can help you when you want to dance:

✔ **La salsa es un baile nuevo.** *(lah sahl-sah ehs oon bvahee-leh nooeh-bvoh)* (The salsa is a new dance.)

✔ **La invito a bailar.** *(lah een-bvee-toh ah bvahee-lahr)* (I invite you [formal, female] to dance.)

✔ **¿Qué clase de bailes habrá?** *(keh klah-seh deh bvahee-lehs ah-bvrah)* (What kind of dances will they have?)

✔ **Habrá salsa, cumbia, un poco de todo. ¡Vamos hasta el reventón!** *(ah-bvrah sahl-sah koom-bveeah oon poh-koh deh toh-doh bvah-mohs ahs-tah ehl reh-bvehn-tohn)* (They'll have salsa, cumbia, a bit of everything. It's going to be a riot! [Literally: We'll go until the blast!])

✔ **Bailamos toda la noche.** *(bvahee-lah-mohs toh-dah lah noh-cheh)* (We danced all night.)

✔ **Bailó hasta la mañana.** *(bvahee-loh ahs-tah lah mah-nyah-nah)* (He/she danced until morning.)

Words to Know

la cumbia	lah <u>koom</u>-bveea	an African-American rhythm
el gusto	ehl <u>goos</u>-toh	the pleasure (Literally: the taste)
el mesón	ehl meh-<u>sohn</u>	old-style bar and restaurant
la ocasión	lah oh-kah-see<u>ohn</u>	the occasion
el reventón	ehl reh-bvehn-<u>tohn</u>	the riotous, noisy party
la salsa	lah <u>sahl</u>-sah	an African-Cuban dance and music rhythm (Literally: the sauce)
el viaje	ehl bveea<u>h</u>-Heh	the trip

Having a Good Time at Shows and Events

The types of events and shows available in Spanish-speaking America vary depending on where they happen. In villages or small towns, the events generally relate to celebrations of important dates, both private and public.

The following list gives you some phrases that can help when you're asked or you're asking to attend an event:

✔ **Voy a buscarte a las ocho**. *(bvohy a bvoos-kahr-teh ah lahs oh-choh)* (I'll pick you up at eight. [Literally: I'll go search you at eight.])

✔ **¡Qué pena, hoy no puedo!** *(keh peh-nah, ohy noh pooeh-doh)* (What a pity, today I can't!)

Screening the cinema

Latin America and Spain have produced rich and varied films. So take the opportunity to see a good Spanish-language film and use some more Spanish:

✔ **Si quieres, vamos al cine.** *(see keeeh-rehs bvah-mohs ahl see-neh)* (If you want, we can go to the movies.)

✔ **¿Hay muchos cines en esta ciudad?** *(ahy moo-chohs see-nehs ehn ehs-tah seeoo-dahd)* (Are there many cinemas in this city?)

✔ **¿Qué dan hoy?** *(keh dahn ohy)* (What's playing today?)

✔ **Veamos la cartelera ¡Ah, mira, la versión original de "Nosferatu"!** *(bveh-ah-mohs lah kahr-teh-leh-rah ah mee-rah lah vehr-seeohn oh-ree-Hee-nahl deh nohs-feh-rah-too)* (Let's see the listings. Look! The original version of Nosferatu!)

✔ **Esta película me gusta.** *(ehs-tah peh-lee-koo-lah meh goos-tah)* (I like this film.)

Enjoying a concert

Going to a concert is a great way to relax and listen to the language — but you have to speak some to get there:

✔ **¿Sabes si viene a cantar Julio Iglesias?** *(sah-bvehs see bveeeh-neh ah kahn-tahr Hoo-leeoh ee-gleh-seeahs)* (Do you know if Julio Iglesias is coming to sing?)

✔ **Quizás. Lo anunciaron.** *(kee-sahs loh ah-noon-seeah-rohn)* (Maybe. They advertised him.)

✔ **Espero que no vaya a cancelar.** *(ehs-peh-roh keh noh bvah ah kahn-seh-lahr)* (I hope he's not going to cancel.)

Sometimes, you're lucky enough to know the people playing your favorite music:

✔ **Sabes, mañana dan un concierto de violín con piano.** *(sah-bvehs mah-nyah-nah dahn oon kohn-seeehr-toh de bvee-oh-leen kohn peeah-noh)* (You know, tomorrow there's going to be a violin and piano concert.)

✔ **¿Quiénes tocan?** *(keeeh-nehs toh-kahn)* (Who's playing?)

✔ **Nuestros amigos Luisa y Fernando.** *(nooehs-trohs ah-mee-gohs looee-sah ee fehr-nahn-doh)* (Our friends Luisa and Fernando.)

✔ **¿Cuál es el programa?** *(kooahl ehs ehl proh-grah-mah)* (What's the program?)

Words to Know

anunciar	ah-noon-seeahr	to advertise; to announce
cancelar	kahn-seh-lahr	to cancel
juntas	Hoon-tahs	together (female)
libre	lee-bvreh	free of charge
la pena	lah peh-nah	sadness; in some countries, shame
el programa	ehl proh-grah-mah	the program
repetir	reh-peh-teer	to repeat

Enjoying the Outdoors

Spanish has two ways to express the idea of going outdoors:

> ✔ **al aire libre** *(ahl ahee-reh lee-bvreh)* (in the open air)
>
> You use this phrase when you're talking about going out to the street, garden, or taking a walk. It implies a feeling of openness and liberty.
>
> ✔ **a la intemperie** *(ah lah een-tehm-peh-reeeh)* (out of doors, exposed to the elements [Literally: in the unheated space])
>
> This phrase implies that you're going to be without a roof nearby and therefore will be suffering or enjoying whatever weather you may find. It gives a feeling of exposure and less safety.

The following examples can help you determine which phrase to use:

> ✔ **Voy a nadar en una piscina al aire libre.** *(bvohy ah nah-dahr ehn oo-nah pee-see-nah ahl ahee-reh lee-bvreh)* (I'm going to swim in an outdoor pool.)
>
> ✔ **No dejes las plantas a la intemperie.** *(noh deh-Hehs lahs plahn-tahs ah lah een-tehm-peh-reeeh)* (Don't leave the plants out in the open.)

Taking a walk

Walking about and enjoying the trees and plants go hand-in-hand. The key verb here is **pasear** *(pah-seh-ahr)* (to walk). The following list shows you some phrases that you may want to use to describe such experiences:

> ✔ **¿Quieres pasear conmigo?** *(keeeh-rehs pah-seh-ahr kohn-mee-goh)* (Would you go on a walk with me?)
>
> ✔ **Me gusta pasear.** *(meh goos-tah pah-seh-ahr)* (I love to walk.)

✔ **Ayer paseamos en la Alameda.** *(ah-yehr pah-seh-ah-mohs ehn lah ah-lah-meh-dah)* (Yesterday, we walked along the Poplar Grove.)

✔ **Hay robles y cipreses.** *(ahy roh-bvlehs ee see-preh-sehs)* (There are oaks and cypresses.)

✔ **Esa palmera da dátiles.** *(eh-sah pahl-meh-rah dah dah-tee-lehs)* (That palm [tree] yields dates.)

✔ **En Chile crecen muchos eucaliptus.** *(ehn chee-leh kreh-sehn moo-chohs ehoo-kah-leep-toos)* (Many eucaluptus [trees] grow in Chile.)

Watching the animals

While on your walk, you probably see a few animals. These phrases get you started talking about animals while you watch them:

✔ **En el paseo vi muchas ardillas.** *(ehn ehl pah-seh-oh bvee moo-chahs ahr-dee-yahs)* (During the walk, I saw many squirrels.)

✔ **En la playa vemos gaviotas.** *(ehn lah plah-yah bveh-mohs gah-bveeoh-tahs)* (On the beach, we see seagulls.)

✔ **En el centro hay muchas palomas.** *(ehn ehl sehn-troh ahy moo-chahs pah-loh-mahs)* (Downtown has many pigeons.)

✔ **Los gorriones se ven en las ciudades.** *(lohs goh-rreeoh-nehs seh bvehn ehn lahs seeoo-dah-dehs)* (The sparrows are seen in the cities.)

✔ **Voy a pasear los perros.** *(bvohy ah pah-seh-ahr lohs peh-rrohs)* (I'm going to walk the dogs.)

✔ **Van a una carrera de caballos.** *(bvahn ah oo-nah kah-rreh-rah deh kah-bvah-yohs)* (They're going to a horse race.)

It would take whole books to talk about animals, but here are a few more examples that you may change to fit your animal-discussion needs:

✔ **El cerro estaba cubierto de mariposas.** *(ehl seh-rroh ehs-tah-bvah koo-bveeehr-toh deh mah-ree-poh-sahs)* (The hill was covered with butterflies.)

✔ **De paseo vi una manada de vacas.** *(deh pah-seh-oh bvee oo-nah mah-nah-dah deh bvah-kahs)* (While walking, I saw a herd of cows.)

✔ **Andamos con unas cabras.** *(ahn-dah-mohs kohn oo-nahs kah-bvrahs)* (We walk with some goats.)

✔ **Cuando pasé me perseguían unos gansos.** *(kooahn-doh pah-seh meh pehr-seh-gheeahn oo-nohs gahn-sohs)* (As I went by, some geese chased me.)

✔ **En el lago vimos patos silvestres.** *(ehn ehl lah-goh bvee-mohs pah-tohs seel-bvehs-trehs)* (We saw wild ducks in the lake.)

✔ **Una señora ¡paseaba un gato!** *(oo-nah seh-nyoh-rah pah-seh-ah-bvah oon gah-toh)* (A lady was walking a cat!)

✔ **La niña llevaba una iguana.** *(lah nee-nyah yeh-bvah-bvah oo-nah ee-gooah-nah)* (The girl was carrying an iguana.)

✔ **Le gusta jugar con el gato.** *(leh goos-tah Hoo-gahr kohn ehl gah-toh)* (She likes to play with the cat.)

Words to Know

la burra	lah bvoo-rrah	the jenny; female burro
la iguana	lah ee-gooah-nah	large lizard, green, with yellow spots, native of Central and South America
		continued

Words to Know (continued)

el mapache	ehl mah-_pah_-cheh	the raccoon
el puma	ehl _poo_-mah	mountain lion
el tucán	ehl too-_kahn_	the toucan, a large, many colored, large-billed bird

Sports, Sports, Sports

Yes, sports are played around the world. But in Latin America and Spain, we're talking holy ground — especially **fútbol.**

The most popular ball game: Fútbol

Yes, **fútbol** (_foot_-bvohl), called "soccer" in North American English and football elsewhere, is the most popular game in Latin America. This game is the talk of taverns, bars, and living rooms, and its stars are national heroes. We dare say there is more talk about **fútbol** in Latin America than about anything else.

Use these phrases to talk shop about this favorite sport:

✔ **Me divierte ver jugar fútbol.** (meh dee-bvee_ehr_-teh bveh Hoo-_gahr_ _foot_-bvohl) (I enjoy watching soccer. [Literally: It amuses me to see soccer.])

✔ **¿Adónde vas a verlo?** (ah-_dohn_-deh bvahs a _bvehr_-loh) (Where do you go to watch it?)

✔ **¿Eres hincha del Boca?** (_eh_-rehs _een_-chah dehl _bvoh_-kah) (Are you a Boca fan?)

✔ **Sí, hace muchos años.** *(see <u>ah</u>-seh <u>moo</u>-chohs <u>ah</u>-nyohs)* (Yes, for many years.)

✔ **¿Qué jugadores te gustan?** *(keh Hoo-gah-<u>doh</u>-rehs teh <u>goos</u>-tahn)* (Which players do you like?)

✔ **Siempre he preferido a los de la defensa.** *(see<u>ehm</u>-preh eh preh-feh-<u>ree</u>-doh ah lohs deh lah deh-<u>fehn</u>-sah)* (I've always preferred those who play defense.)

✔ **¿Y no te gustan los centro delanteros?** *(ee noh teh <u>goos</u>-tahn lohs <u>sehn</u>-troh deh-lahn-<u>teh</u>-rohs)* (You don't like the center forwards?)

Words to Know

el arquero	ehl ahr-<u>keh</u>-roh	the goalkeeper (arco [<u>ahr</u>-koh] means "arch")
la cancha	lah <u>kahn</u>-chah	the playing field
el defensa	ehl deh-<u>fehn</u>-sah	the defense
los delanteros	lohs deh-lahn-<u>teh</u>-rohs	the forwards
divertir	dee-bvehr-<u>teer</u>	to amuse
el equipo	ehl eh-<u>kee</u>-poh	the team
el estadio	ehl ehs-<u>tah</u>-deeoh	the stadium
ganar	gah-<u>nahr</u>	to win
el gol	ehl gohl	the hit, goal

continued

Words to Know (continued)

el hincha	ehl _een_-chah	the fan (hincha [een-chahr] means to inflate, to bloat)
el jugador	ehl Hoo-gah-_dohr_	the player
el rol	ehl rohl	the role

Béisbol: #2

El béisbol _(ehl bveh̲ees-bvohl)_ (baseball) is definitely the second most important ball game (after **fútbol**) in Mexico, Central America, and the Caribbean.

The following phrases describe a recent baseball game:

🖙 **Ese tipo batea de maravilla.** _(eh-seh tee̲-poh bvah-teh̲-ah deh mah-rah-bvee̲-yah)_ (That guy's a wonder at bat.)

🖙 **E hizo una carrera estupenda.** _(eh ee̲-soh oo̲-nah kah-rreh̲-rah ehs-too-pehn̲-dah)_ (And he did a stupendous run.)

🖙 **No podía creer cuando llegó a la goma. . .** _(noh poh-dee̲ah kreh̲-ehr kooah̲n-doh yeh-goh̲ ah lah goh̲-mah)_ (I couldn't believe it when he made it to home plate. . .)

🖙 **. . . y eso que antes era un juego con once hits.** _(ee eh̲-soh keh ah̲n-tehs eh̲-rah oon Hoo̲eh-goh kohn ohn̲-seh Heets)_ (. . . and before that it was a game with 11 hits.)

Words to Know

batear	bvah-teh-<u>ahr</u>	to bat
la carrera	lah kah-<u>rreh</u>-rah	the run, the race
la goma	lah <u>goh</u>-mah	the home base (Literally: the rubber)

The playing verb: Jugar

Jugar *(Hoo-<u>gahr</u>)* (to play) is a slightly irregular verb, but it's a very playful and useful one — definitely worth the effort, so check out Table 7-1.

Table 7-1	Jugar
Conjugation	*Pronunciation*
yo juego	yoh Hoo<u>eh</u>-goh
tú juegas	too Hoo<u>eh</u>-gahs
él, ella, ello, uno, usted juega	ehl, <u>eh</u>-yah, <u>eh</u>-yoh, <u>oo</u>-noh, oos-<u>tehd</u>, Hoo<u>eh</u>-gah
nosotros jugamos	noh-<u>soh</u>-trohs Hoo-<u>gah</u>-mohs
vosotros jugáis	bvoh-<u>soh</u>-trohs Hoo-<u>gah</u>-ees
ellos, ellas, ustedes juegan	<u>eh</u>-yohs, <u>eh</u>-yahs, oos-<u>teh</u>-dehs Hoo<u>eh</u>-gahn

Practicing your game a little is always good. The following phrases can help when you play:

- ✔ **¿Jugamos béisbol hoy?** *(Hoo-gah-mohs bvehees-bvohl ohy)* (Are we playing baseball today?)

- ✔ **Juega mejor que hace un mes.** *(Hooeh-gah meh-Hohr keh ah-seh oon mehs)* ([He] plays better than a month ago.)

Chapter 8

When You Gotta Work

- -

In This Chapter
▶ Conversing by phone
▶ Describing your office
▶ Conducting business

- -

Making an effort with your Spanish-speaking business associates or clients will impress them — who knows, maybe it will seal the deal. This chapter helps you navigate the basics of business activities.

Picking Up the Phone

Making — or receiving — a phone call in Spanish can be nerve wracking, but the best thing to do is take a deep breath, and don't hesitate to ask the person on the other end to repeat himself.

Opening lines

So you punch in or dial a phone number — then what?

- ✔ Argentinians say **¡Holá!** (*oh<u>lah</u>*)
- ✔ Chileans say **¡Aló!** (*ah-<u>loh</u>*)
- ✔ Mexicans say **¡Bueno!** (*bvoo<u>eh</u>-noh*)
- ✔ In Spain, you hear **¡Sí!** (*see*)

These words all mean, "Hello!" Most Spanish-speaking countries use **aló,** in the Chilean way.

These phrases come in very handy when you use the phone:

- **llamar por teléfono** *(yah-mahr pohr teh-leh-foh-noh)* (make a phone call)
- **marcar el número** *(mahr-kahr ehl noo-meh-roh)* (dial/punch in the number)
- **colgar** *(kohl-gahr)* (hang up)
- **la línea está libre** *(lah lee-nee-ah ehs-tah lee-bvreh)* (the line is open)
- **la línea está ocupada** *(lah lee-neh-ah ehs-tah oh-koo-pah-dah)* (the line is busy)
- **el teléfono no responde** *(ehl teh-leh-foh-noh noh rehs-pohn-deh)* (there's no answer)

Words to Know

llamar	yah-mahr	to call
marcar	mahr-kahr	to mark; to dial; to punch in the number
el número	ehl noo-meh-roh	the number
colgar	kohl-gahr	to hang; to hang up
la línea	lah lee-neh-ah	the line
libre	lee-bvreh	free
ocupada	oh-koo-pah-dah	busy (female)
responder	rehs-pohn-dehr	to answer

Take a look at these handy phrases, which you can use when you're having trouble hearing:

✔ **¡Bueno! ¿Hablo con Juanita?** *(bvoo__eh__-noh ah-bvloh kohn Hooah-__nee__-tah)* (Hello! Am I speaking to Juanita?)

✔ **Perdone, no le escucho.** *(pehr-__doh__-neh noh leh ehs-__koo__-choh)* (Excuse me, I can't hear you.)

✔ **Está muy mala la línea, ¿lo repite por favor?** *(ehs-__tah__ mooy __mah__-lah lah __lee__-neh-ah loh reh-__pee__-teh pohr fah-__bvohr__)* (The line is very bad, will you please repeat what you said?)

Words to Know

hablar	ah-_bvlahr_	to talk
escuchar	ehs-koo-_chahr_	to listen; to hear
dejar	deh-_Hahr_	to leave (a message)
más tarde	mahs _tahr_-deh	later
en la tarde	ehn lah _tahr_-deh	in the afternoon

Leaving messages

The following phrases help you understand that the person you're calling isn't available and show you how to leave a message for the person you missed:

✔ **En este momento no está.** *(ehn __ehs__-teh moh-__mehn__-toh noh ehs-__tah__)* (She's not here at the moment.)

✔ **Llamo más tarde, gracias.** *(__yah__-moh mahs __tahr__-deh __grah__-seeahs)* (I'll call later, thanks.)

✔ **Quisiera dejar un mensaje.** *(kee-seee_eh_-rah deh-_Hahr_ oon mehn-_sah_-Heh)* (I would like to leave a message.)

✔ **El mensaje es que . . .** *(ehl mehn-_sah_-Heh ehs keh)* (The message is that . . .)

✔ **¿Me puede repetir su apellido, por favor?** *(meh pooe_h_-deh reh-peh-_teer_ soo ah-peh-_yee_-doh pohr fah-_bvohr_)* (Can you repeat your last name, please?)

✔ **¿Cómo se escribe?** *(_koh_-moh seh ehs-_kree_-bveh)* (How do you spell it?)

If you missed a call, you may hear the following:

✔ **Te llamaron por teléfono.** *(teh yah-_mah_-rohn pohr teh-_leh_-foh-noh)* (You had a phone call.)

✔ **Le llamé ayer.** *(leh yah-_meh_ ah-_yehr_)* (I called you [formal] yesterday.)

✔ **Ayer no me llamaste.** *(ah-_yehr_ noh meh yah-_mahs_-teh)* (Yesterday you [informal] didn't call me.)

✔ **Cuando te llamé me colgaron.** *(kooa_hn_-doh teh yah-_meh_ meh kohl-_gah_-rohn)* (When I called you [informal], they hung up on me. [Literally: They hung me up.])

✔ **Te dejé un recado.** *(teh deh-_Heh_ oon reh-_kah_-doh)* (I left you a message.)

✔ **¿Dejaste un mensaje largo?** *(deh-_Hahs_-teh oon mehn-_sah_-Heh _lahr_-goh)* (Did you [informal] leave a long message?)

✔ **El mensaje que dejaron es breve.** *(ehl mehn-_sah_-Heh keh deh-_Hah_-rohn ehs _bvreh_-bveh)* (The message they left is brief.)

✔ **Dejó el número de teléfono.** *(deh-_Hoh_ ehl _noo_-meh-roh deh teh-_leh_-foh-noh)* (She left the telephone number.)

Making a collect call

If you're short on change, knowing these phrases can help you make a collect call:

- ✔ **¡Bueno!, operadora, quisiera hacer una llamada por cobrar.** *(bvoo<u>eh</u>-noh oh-peh-rah-<u>doh</u>-rah kee-see<u>eh</u>-rah <u>ah</u>-sehr <u>oo</u>-nah lyah-<u>mah</u>-dah pohr koh-<u>bvrahr</u>)* (Hello, operator, I'd like to make a collect call.)

- ✔ **¿A qué número?** *(ah keh <u>noo</u>-meh-roh)* (To what number?)

- ✔ **¿Y el código del área?** *(ee ehl <u>koh</u>-dee-goh dehl <u>ah</u>-reh-ah)* (And the area code?)

- ✔ **¿Cómo se llama usted?** *(<u>koh</u>-moh seh <u>yah</u>-mah oos-<u>tehd</u>)* (What's your name?)

- ✔ **La línea no responde. Llame más tarde, por favor.** *(lah <u>lee</u>-neh-ah noh rehs-<u>pohn</u>-deh <u>yah</u>-meh mahs <u>tahr</u>-deh pohr fah-<u>bvohr</u>)* (The line doesn't answer. Call later, please.)

Outside the Office

Here are some words and phrases that you can use to describe your office and other buildings:

- ✔ **edificio de oficinas** *(eh-dee-<u>fee</u>-seeoh deh oh-fee-<u>see</u>-nahs)* (office building)

- ✔ **edificio de muchos pisos** *(eh-dee-<u>fee</u>-seeoh deh <u>moo</u>-chohs <u>pee</u>-sohs)* (building with many floors; high-rise)

- ✔ **edificio alto** *(eh-dee-<u>fee</u>-seeoh <u>ahl</u>-toh)* (tall building; high-rise)

- ✔ **edificio de torre** *(eh-dee-<u>fee</u>-seeoh deh <u>toh</u>-rreh)* (a tower building)

- ✔ **edificio de una planta** *(eh-dee-<u>fee</u>-seeoh deh <u>oo</u>-nah <u>plahn</u>-tah)* (one-story building)

Practice building terms with the following phrases:

✔ **El edificio de Correos tiene siete pisos.** *(ehl eh-dee-fee-seeoh deh koh-rreh-ohs tee-eh-neh see-eh-teh pee-sohs)* (The Postal building is seven stories high.)

✔ **La oficina está en un edificio de dos pisos.** *(lah oh-fee-see-nah ehs-tah ehn oon eh-dee-fee-seeoh deh dohs pee-sohs)* (The office is in a two-story building.)

✔ **Busco el edificio de oficinas fiscales.** *(bvoos-koh ehl eh-dee-fee-seeoh deh oh-fee-see-nahs fees-kah-lehs)* (I'm looking for the building of public revenues.)

✔ **Vamos a un edificio muy alto.** *(bvah-mohs a oon eh-dee-fee-seeoh mooy ahl-toh)* (We're going to a very tall building.)

✔ **En ese edificio sólo hay oficinas.** *(ehn eh-seh eh-dee-fee-seeoh soh-loh ahy oh-fee-see-nahs)* (This building only has offices.)

✔ **Tres plantas de ese edificio son de la compañía.** *(trehs plahn-tahs deh eh-seh eh-dee-fee-seeoh sohn deh lah kohm-pah-nyeeah)* (Three floors in that building belong to the company.)

Words to Know

el edificio	ehl eh-dee-fee-seeoh	the building
el piso	ehl pee-soh	the floor
la planta baja	lah plahn-tah bvah-Hah	the floor at ground level
alto	ahl-toh	tall; high

Inside the Office

Conversations about jobs, workplaces, and offices don't differ much from one language to another. Table 8-1 lists some Spanish terms that can help you talk about life on the job:

Table 8-1	Life on the Job Words	
Spanish	*Pronunciation*	*English*
el empleo	ehl ehm-<u>pleh</u>-oh	the job; employment
presentarse	preh-sehn-<u>tahr</u>-seh	to go to be present at some place; to introduce oneself
la entrevista	lah ehn-treh-<u>bvees</u>-tah	the interview
el personal	ehl pehr-soh-<u>nahl</u>	the staff; the personnel
el ascensor	ehl ah-sehn-<u>sohr</u>	the elevator
el pasillo	ehl pah-<u>see</u>-yoh	the corridor; the aisle
la cita	lah <u>see</u>-tah	the appointment; the date [as in going on a date with someone]
la secretaria	lah seh-kreh-<u>tah</u>-reeah	the female secretary
el secretario	ehl seh-kreh-<u>tah</u>-reeoh	the male secretary
gerencial	Heh-rehn-see-<u>ahl</u>	managerial
antes	<u>ahn</u>-tehs	before

(continued)

Table 8-1 *(continued)*

Spanish	Pronunciation	English
la carta	lah <u>kahr</u>-tah	the letter
la recomendación	lah reh-koh-mehn-dah-see-<u>ohn</u>	the recommendation

Getting a job

Interested in working in a Spanish-speaking environment? Here's how an interview can go:

- ✔ **¿Tiene experiencia con computadoras?** *(teeeh-neh ehks-peh-ree<u>ehn</u>-seeah kohn kom-poo-tah-<u>doh</u>-rahs)* (Do you have experience with computers?)

- ✔ **Sí, tengo cinco años de experiencia.** *(see <u>tehn</u>-goh <u>seen</u>-koh <u>ah</u>-nyos deh ehks-peh-ree-<u>ehn</u>-seeah)* (Yes, I have five years' experience.)

- ✔ **¿Qué trabajo ha hecho con computadoras?** *(keh trah-<u>bvah</u>-Hoh ah <u>eh</u>-choh kohn kohm-poo-tah-<u>doh</u>-rahs)* (What work did you do with computers?)

- ✔ **He trabajado en captura de datos y también en procesar textos.** *(eh trah-bvah-<u>Hah</u>-doh ehn kahp-<u>too</u>-rah de <u>dah</u>-tohs ee tahm-bvee<u>ehn</u> ehn proh-seh-<u>sahr</u> <u>tehks</u>-tohs)* (I've done data processing, as well as word processing.)

- ✔ **¿Le ha tocado hacer diseño?** *(leh ah toh-<u>kah</u>-doh <u>ah</u>-sehr dee-<u>seh</u>-nyoh)* (Have you done any design?)

- ✔ **¿Maneja usted el correo electrónico?** *(mah-<u>neh</u>-Hah <u>oos</u>-tehd ehl koh-<u>rreh</u>-oh eh-lehk-<u>troh</u>-nee-koh)* (Do you handle e-mail?)

- ✔ **Sí. También manejo otros programas. Mi anterior jefe era diseñador de programas.** *(see tahm-bvee<u>ehn</u> mah-<u>neh</u>-Hoh <u>oh</u>-trohs proh-<u>grah</u>-mahs mee ahn-teh-ree-<u>ohr</u> <u>Heh</u>-feh <u>eh</u>-rah dee-seh-nyah-<u>dohr</u> deh proh-<u>grah</u>-mahs)* (Yes, and also other programs. My previous boss was a programmer.)

Words to Know

la computadora	lah kohm-poo-tah-<u>doh</u>-rah	the computer
la captura	lah kahp-<u>too</u>-rah	the capture (in computer speak: processing)
los textos	lohs <u>teks</u>-tohs	the texts (in computer speak: words)
el diseño	ehl dee-<u>seh</u>-nyoh	the design
el curso	ehl <u>koor</u>-soh	the course
manejar	mah-neh-<u>Hahr</u>	to handle; to drive (a car)
programar	proh-grah-<u>mahr</u>	to program; to make software
el programa	ehl proh-<u>grah</u>-mah	the software

Sometimes, you can find a job through hearsay. In the following dialog, several positions are open in a furniture factory:

- ✔ **En esa fábrica emplean gente.** *(ehn <u>eh</u>-sah <u>fah</u>-bvree-kah ehm-<u>pleh</u>-ahn <u>Hehn</u>-teh)* (That factory is hiring.

- ✔ **¿Qué producen allí?** *(keh proh-<u>doo</u>-sehn ahee)* (What do they make there?)

- ✔ **¿Qué empleos ofrecen?** *(keh ehm-<u>pleohs</u> oh-<u>freh</u>-sehn)* (What jobs do they have open?)

✔ **Hay un empleo de oficina y otro en la planta.**
(ahy oon ehm-pleh-oh deh oh-fee-see-nah ee oh-troh ehn lah plahn-tah) (There's an office job and another in the shop.)

✔ **¿Por qué no pides información?** *(pohr keh noh pee-dehs een-fohr-mah-see-ohn)* (Why don't you ask for information?)

Words to Know

la fábrica	lah fah-bvree-kah	the factory
producir	proh-doo-seer	to produce; to make
el empleo	ehl ehm-pleh-oh	the employment; the job
emplear	ehm-pleh-ahr	to employ; to hire
la planta	lah plahn-tah	the plant (as in a factory)
interesar	een-teh-reh-sahr	to interest
pedir	peh-deer	to ask for
ofrecer	oh-freh-sehr	to offer

Scheduling and conducting a meeting

If you need to schedule a meeting, these phrases can help you out:

✔ **Quiero organizar una reunión para el miércoles.** *(keeeh-roh ohr-gah-nee-sahr oo-nah rehoo-neeohn pah-rah ehl meeehr-koh-lehs)* (I want to arrange a meeting for Wednesday.)

✔ **Usted tiene disponible dos horas en la tarde.**
(oos-tehd teeeh-neh dees-poh-nee-bvleh dohs oh-rahs ehn lah tahr-deh) (You have two hours available in the afternoon.)

✔ **Bien. Póngala en la sala de conferencias.**
(bveeehn pohn-gah-lah ehn lah sah-lah deh kohn-feh-rehn-seeahs) (Good. Schedule it for the conference room.)

✔ **Avise por fax a mi socio, por favor y recuérdeme el día antes.** *(ah-bvee-seh pohr fahks ah mee soh-seeoh pohr fah-bvohr ee reh-koo-ehr-deh-meh ehl deeah ahn-tehs)* (Please let my partner know, via fax, and remind me the day before.)

Words to Know

el archivo	ehl ahr-chee-bvoh	the file
la base de datos	lah bvah-seh de dah-tohs	the data base
imprimir	eem-pree-meer	to print
teclear	tehk-leh-ahr	to type
el teclado	ehl tehk-lah-doh	the keyboard
enviar	ehn-bvee-ahr	to send
quedarse	keh-dahr-seh	to stay
el compromiso	ehl kohm-proh-mee-soh	the commitment; ment; the engagement; plans
el informe	ehl een-fohr-meh	the report
junto	Hoon-toh	together

When it comes time for your meeting, you may use phrases similar to these:

- **Señores, ante todo agradezco su presencia.** *(seh-nyoh-rehs ahn-teh toh-doh ah-grah-dehs-koh soo preh-sehn-seeah)* (Ladies and gentlemen, I first want to thank you for coming.)

- **Estamos aquí por un asunto de importancia. Estamos considerando este contrato.** *(ehs-tah-mohs ah-kee-pohr oon ah-soon-toh deh eem-pohr-tahn-seeah ehs-tah-mohs kohn-see-deh-rahn-doh ehs-teh kohn-trah-toh)* (We're here for an important matter: We're considering this contract.)

- **¿Se ha firmado algo ya?** *(seh ah feer-mah-doh ahl-goh yah)* (Has anything been signed yet?)

- **Quiero consultar con ustedes primero y también quiero consultar con nuestros abogados.** *(keeeh-roh kohn-sool-tahr kohn oos-teh-dehs pree-meh-roh ee tahm-bveeehn keeeh-roh kohn-sool-tahr kohn nooehs-trohs ah-bvoh-gah-dohs)* (I want to consult with you first, and I also want to consult with our lawyers.)

- **Tome nota para las actas de la reunión.** *(toh-meh noh-tah pah-rah lahs ahk-tahs deh lah rehoo-neeohn)* (Take minutes of the meeting.)

Words to Know

el asunto	ehl ah-soon-toh	the matter
firmar	feer-mahr	to sign
consultar	koh-sool-tahr	to consult
el abogado	ehl ah-bvoh-gah-doh	the lawyer
grabar	grah-bvahr	to tape

Using emplear: The hiring verb

Emplear *(ehm-pleh-ahr)* (to employ; to hire; to use) is a multifaceted verb. This regular verb uses the root **emple-** *(ehm-pleh)*. See Chapter 2 for the conjugation of regular verbs.

Here are some phrases to help you practice using emplear:

- ✔ **La fábrica emplea cincuenta operarios.** *(lah fah-bvree-kah ehm-pleh-ah seen-koo-ehn-tah oh-peh-rah-reeohs)* (The factory employs 50 workers.)

- ✔ **Nosotros empleamos dos horas en el trabajo.** *(noh-soh-trohs ehm-pleh-ah-mohs dohs oh-rahs ehn ehl trah-bvah-Hoh)* (It took us two hours to do the work.)

- ✔ **Van a emplearlos en un taller.** *(bvahn ah ehm-pleh-ahr-lohs ehn oon tah-yehr)* (They're going to hire them in a [work]shop.)

- ✔ **Esa computadora se emplea para diseñar.** *(eh-sah kohm-poo-tah-doh-rah seh ehm-pleh-ah pah-rah dee-seh-nyahr)* (That computer is used for design work.)

- ✔ **Queremos emplear personas responsables.** *(keh-reh-mohs ehm-pleh-ahr pehr-soh-nahs rehs-pohn-sah-bvlehs)* (We want to employ responsible people.)

- ✔ **Emplean sólo personas de confianza.** *(ehm-pleh-ahn soh-loh pehr-soh-nahs deh kohn-feeahn-sah)* (They only employ dependable people.)

- ✔ **La emplean porque es persona con quien se puede contar.** *(lah ehm-pleh-ahn pohr-keh ehs pehr-soh-nah kohn keeehn seh pooeh-deh kohn-tahr)* (They employ her because they can count on her.)

Hacer: The doing, making verb

Like most of the verbs that you have to use frequently, **hacer** *(ah-sehr)* (to do; to make) is a very irregular verb, changing its root from pronoun to pronoun and from tense to tense.

Hacer's root, **hac-,** transforms and deforms itself within the first person singular. Table 8-2 conjugates **hacer** in the present tense:

Table 8-2	Hacer
Conjugation	*Pronunciation*
yo hago	yoh <u>ah</u>-goh
tú haces	too <u>ah</u>-sehs
él, ella, ello, uno, usted hace	ehl <u>eh</u>-yah <u>eh</u>-yoh <u>oo</u>-noh, oos-<u>tehd</u> <u>ah</u>-seh
nosotros hacemos	noh-<u>soh</u>-trohs ah-<u>seh</u>-mohs
vosotros hacéis	bvoh-<u>soh</u>-trohs ah-<u>seh</u>ees
ellos, ellas, ustedes hacen	<u>eh</u>-yohs <u>eh</u>-yahs oos-<u>teh</u>-dehs <u>ah</u>-sehn

Here are some phrases that you may use with the verb **hacer:**

- ✔ **Carlos hace muebles.** *(<u>kahr</u>-lohs <u>ah</u>-seh moo<u>eh</u>-bvlehs)* (Carlos makes furniture.)

- ✔ **Nosotros hacemos nuestro pan.** *(noh-<u>soh</u>-trohs ah-<u>seh</u>-mohs noo<u>ehs</u>-troh pahn)* (We make our own bread.)

- ✔ **Todos hacen cola.** *(<u>toh</u>-dohs <u>ah</u>-sehn <u>koh</u>-lah)* (They all line up. [Literally: They all make a tail.])

- ✔ **Tú haces mucha comida.** *(too <u>ah</u>-sehs <u>moo</u>-chah koh-<u>mee</u>-dah)* (You make a lot of food.)

- ✔ **No tiene nada que hacer.** *(noh tee<u>eh</u>-neh <u>nah</u>-dah keh <u>ah</u>-sehr)* (He has nothing to do.)

- ✔ **No hacemos nada malo.** *(noh ah-<u>seh</u>-mohs <u>nah</u>-dah <u>mah</u>-loh)* (We're doing no harm [Literally: bad].)

- ✔ **Ignacio hace casas de adobe.** *(eeg-<u>nah</u>-seeoh <u>ah</u>-seh <u>kah</u>-sahs deh ah-<u>doh</u>-bveh)* (Ignacio makes adobe houses.)

✔ **Rosa María hace bellos jardines.** (*roh*-sah mah-*reeah* *ah*-seh *bveh*-yohs Har-*dee*-nehs) (Rosa María makes beautiful gardens.)

Packing a PC

Computers are a part of everyday life. Here are some phrases that can help when talking about your computer:

✔ **Voy a llevar conmigo la computadora portátil.** (*bvohy* ah yeh-*bvahr* kohn-*mee*-goh lah kohm-poo-tah-*doh*-rah pohr-*tah*-teel) (I'll take the laptop computer.)

✔ **No te olvides las baterías.** (noh teh ohl-*bvee*-dehs lahs bah-teh-*ree*-ahs) (Don't forget the batteries.)

✔ **Vas a llevar el adaptador de corriente.** (*bvahs* a yeh-*bvahr* ehl ah-dahp-tah-*dohr* deh koh-rreeehn-teh) (You will take the voltage adapter.)

✔ **Necesitamos el adaptador para cargar la batería.** (neh-seh-see-*tah*-mohs ehl ah-dahp-tah-*dohr* *pah*-rah *kahr*-gahr la bah-teh-*ree*-ah) (We need the adapter to charge the battery.)

Words to Know

la computadora portátil	lah **kohm**-poo-tah-**doh**-rah pohr-**tah**-teel	laptop computer
la batería	lah bah-teh-**ree**-ah	battery
la corriente	lah koh-rree**ehn**-teh	current
cargar	kahr-**gahr**	to charge

Chapter 9

I Get Around: Transportation

- -

In This Chapter

▶ Navigating public transportation

▶ Going through customs

▶ Getting and giving directions

- -

Getting where you want to go in a Spanish-speaking country or trying to help Spanish speakers navigate your own neighborhood pretty much requires you to use your Spanish. This chapter gives you the goods on finding transportation — and finding directions.

On the Go: Transportation

This section gets you on the right train or bus. It also guides you through catching a taxi and renting a car.

Boarding the train

First, you have to get to the train station; these phrases can help:

✔ **¿Dónde está la estación del tren?** (*dohn-deh ehs-tah lah ehs-tah-seeohn dehl trehn*) (Where's the train station?)

✔ **¿Cómo llego a la Estación Central?** *(koh-moh yeh-goh ah lah ehs-tah-seeohn sehn-trahl)* (How do I get to the Central Station?)

✔ **Lléveme por favor a la estación del tren.** *(yeh-bveh-meh pohr fah-bvohr ah lah ehs-tah-seeohn dehl trehn)* (Please take me to the train station.)

After you're there, you need to get a ticket:

✔ **Un boleto para La Paz, por favor.** *(oon bvoh-leh-toh pah-rah lah pahs pohr fah-bvohr)* (One ticket for La Paz, please.)

✔ **¿Primera, segunda o tercera clase?** *(pree-meh-rah seh-goohn-dah oh tehr-seh-rah klah-seh)* (First, second, or third class?)

✔ **¿A qué hora sale el tren?** *(ah keh oh-rah sah-leh ehl trehn)* (What time does the train leave?)

✔ **Sale diez minutos atrasado, a las 12:15.** *(sah-leh deeehs mee-noo-tohs ah-trah-sah-doh ah lahs doh-seh keen-seh)* (It leaves ten minutes late, at 12:15.)

✔ **¿De qué andén sale?** *(deh keh ahn-dehn sah-leh)* (What platform does it leave from?)

✔ **Del andén número dos.** *(dehl ahn-dehn noo-meh-roh dohs)* (From Platform Two.)

Words to Know

la estación	lah ehs-tah-seeohn	the station
el tren	ehl trehn	the train
el boleto	ehl bvoh-leh-toh	the ticket
primera clase	pree-meh-rah klah-seh	first class
el asiento	ehl ah-seeehn-toh	the seat

Hailing a taxi

Whether you're just arriving by plane or your car is in the shop, you may need to search for a taxi at some point. These phrases help you make the arrangements you need:

✔ **¿Dónde encuentro un taxi?** *(dohn-deh ehn-kooehn-troh oon tah-ksee)* (Where do I find a taxi?)

✔ **¿Hay paraderos de taxis?** *(ahy pah-rah-deh-rohs deh tah-ksees)* (Is there a taxi stop?)

✔ **¿Se paga aquí el taxi?** *(seh pah-gah ah-kee ehl tah-ksee)* (Do I pay the taxi here?)

✔ **No. El taxi se paga al llegar a su destino.** *(noh ehl tah-ksee seh pah-gah ahl yeh-gahr ah soo dehs-tee-noh)* (No. You pay the taxi when you arrive at your destination.)

Hopping a bus

Here are some phrases that are useful to know when you need to take a bus:

✔ **¿Hay paraderos de buses?** *(ahy pah-rah-deh-rohs deh bvoo-sehs)* (Is there a bus stop?)

✔ **¿Hay buses para ir al centro?** *(ahy bvoo-sehs pah-rah eer ahl sehn-troh)* (Are there buses for downtown?)

✔ **¿Aquí para el bus de Palermo?** *(ah-kee pah-rah ehl bvoos deh pah-lehr-moh)* (Does the Palermo bus stop here?)

✔ **¿Qué bus tomo para Caballito?** *(keh bvoos toh-moh pah-rah kah-bvah-yee-toh)* (What bus do I take for Caballito?)

✔ **¿A qué calle va?** *(ah keh kah-yeh bvah)* (What street are you going to?)

✔ **¿El cuarenta me deja en Rivadavia con La Rural?** *(ehl kooah-rehn-tah meh deh-Hah ehn ree-bvah-dah-bveeah kohn lah roo-rahl)* (Does [bus] number 40 leave me at Rivadavia and La Rural?)

✔ **Le dejo cerca. Suba.** *(leh deh-Hoh sehr-kah. soo-bvah)* (I'll leave you close. Come on up.)

✔ **¿Se compran los boletos antes?** *(seh kohm-prahn lohs bvoh-leh-tohs ahn-tehs)* (Do I buy the tickets beforehand?)

Words to Know

el paradero	ehl pah-rah-deh-roh	the stop
se paga	seh pah-gah	one pays
la calle	lah kah-yeh	the street
el camión	ehl kah-mee-ohn	the bus [in Mexico]
el trolebús	ehl troh-leh-bvoos	the trolley bus
el trolley	ehl troh-ley	the trolley bus
la micro	lah mee-kroh	the bus [in Chile]
el bus	ehl bvoos	the bus
cerca	sehr-kah	close by

Renting a car

If you need to rent a car, these two questions can come in handy:

✔ **¿Dónde arriendan autos?** *(dohn-deh ah-rreeehn-dahn ahoo-tohs)* (Where do they rent cars?)

✔ **¿Hay oficina de renta de autos?** *(ahy oh-fee-see-nah deh rehn-tah deh ahoo-tohs)* (Is there a car rental office?)

Now you come to the nitty-gritty of trying to rent a car. Here are some things that you can say when inquiring about a rental car:

> ✔ **Quiero arrendar un auto.** *(keeeh-roh ah-rrehn-dahr oon ahoo-toh)* (I want to rent a car.)

> ✔ **¿Me puede dar la lista de precios?** *(meh pooeh-deh dahr lah lees-tah deh preh-seeohs)* (Can you give me the price list?)

> ✔ **¿Cuánto cuesta al día?** *(kooahn-toh kooehs-tah ahl dee-ah)* (How much is it per day?)

> ✔ **¿Cuánto cuesta por semana?** *(kooahn-toh kooehs-tah pohr seh-mah-nah)* (How much is it per week?)

> ✔ **¿Cuántos kilómetros puedo andar?** *(kooahn-tohs kee-loh-meh-trohs pooeh-doh ahn-dahr)* (How many kilometers may I go?)

> ✔ **¿Cuánto cuesta el seguro?** *(kooahn-toh kooehs-tah ehl seh-goo-roh)* (How much is the insurance?)

> ✔ **¿Tiene mapas de la región?** *(teeeh-neh mah-pahs deh lah reh-Heeohn)* (Do you have maps of the region?)

> ✔ **¿Dónde tengo que devolver el auto?** *(dohn-deh tehn-goh keh deh-bvohl-bvehr ehl ahoo-toh)* (Where do I have to return the car?)

You also want to know about the car you're renting and the driving conditions. These phrases can help you get the information that you need:

> ✔ **¿El auto es estándar o automático?** *(ehl ahoo-toh ehs ehs-tahn-dahr oh ahoo-toh-mah-tee-koh)* (Is the car standard or automatic?)

> ✔ **¿Cuántos kilómetros por litro da este auto?** *(kooahn-tohs kee-loh-meh-trohs pohr lee-tro dah ehs-teh ahoo-toh)* (How many kilometers per liter does this car make?)

✔ **¿Dónde está la rueda de repuesto?** *(dohn-deh ehs-tah lah rooeh-dah deh reh-pooehs-toh)* (Where's the spare tire?)

✔ **¿Es difícil manejar por aquí?** *(ehs dee-fee-seel mah-neh-Hahr pohr ah-kee)* (Is it hard to drive around here?)

✔ **Hay que tener mucha prudencia.** *(ahy keh teh-nehr moo-chah proo-dehn-seeah)* (You have to be very prudent/careful.)

✔ **¿Habrá mucho tráfico en la mañana?** *(ah-bvrah moo-choh trah-fee-koh ehn lah mah-nyah-nah)* (Will there be much traffic in the morning?)

✔ **¿Cuál es la mejor hora para salir de la ciudad?** *(kooahl ehs lah meh-Hohr oh-rah pah-rah sah-leer deh lah seeoo-dahd)* (What is the best time to get out of the city?)

The people at the car rental office may know something about the roads that you don't. Here are some questions and answers that you may get while the agent and you are looking at a map:

✔ **¿Están pavimentados los caminos?** *(ehs-tahn pah-bvee-mehn-tah-dohs lohs kah-mee-nohs)* (Are the roads paved?)

✔ **No todos. Estos son de tierra.** (**terracería** [Mexico]). *(noh toh-dohs ehs-tohs sohn deh teeeh-rrah [teh-rrah-seh-reeah])* (Not all of them. These are dirt roads.)

✔ **Esos caminos tienen muchos baches.** *(eh-sohs kah-mee-nohs teeeh-nehn moo-chohs bvah-chehs)* (Those roads have a lot of potholes.)

✔ **Esos caminos son excelentes.** *(eh-sohs kah-mee-nohs sohn ehk-seh-lehn-tehs)* (Those roads are excellent.)

✔ **Hay autopista.** *(ahy ahoo-toh-pees-tah)* (There's a freeway.)

✔ **Son caminos de peaje.** (**cuotas** [Mexico]). *(sohn kah-mee-nohs deh peh-ah-Heh [koooh-tahs])* (They're toll roads.)

Words to Know

arriendan	ah-rree<u>ehn</u>-dahn	they rent
renta	<u>rehn</u>-tah	rental
el camino	ehl kah-<u>mee</u>-noh	the road
el pavimento	ehl pah-bvee-<u>mehn</u>-toh	the pavement
de tierra	deh tee<u>eh</u>-rrah	dirt [road]
de terracería	deh teh-rrah-seh-<u>ree</u>ah	dirt [road]
la autopista	lah ahoo-toh-<u>pees</u>-tah	the freeway
la cuota	lah koo<u>oh</u>-tah	the toll [Mexico]
el peaje	ehl <u>pehah</u>-Heh	the toll
manejar	mah-neh-<u>Hahr</u>	to drive
los reglamentos	lohs rehg-lah-<u>mehn</u>-tohs	the rules
doblar	doh-<u>bvlahr</u>	to turn
salir	sah-<u>leer</u>	to exit

Passing Passport Control

Whenever you cross an international border, you have to go through passport control. If you're entering a country by train, the ticket collector comes at some moment and says such things as:

✔ **¿Me permiten sus pasaportes por favor?** *(meh pehr-mee-tehn soos pah-sah-pohr-tehs pohr fah-bvohr)* (May I have your passports, please?)

✔ **Me llevo sus pasaportes un rato.** *(meh yeh-bvoh soos pah-sah-pohr-tehs oon rah-toh)* (I'll take your passports for a while.)

✔ **Aquí tienen de vuelta sus pasaportes.** *(ah-kee teeeh-nehn deh bvooehl-tah soos pah-sah-pohr-tehs)* (Here are your passports back.)

✔ **Aquí tienen sus formularios de Aduana.** *(ah-kee teeeh-nehn soos fohr-moo-lah-reeohs deh ah-dooah-nah)* (Here are your Customs forms.)

✔ **Llenen por favor el cuestionario.** *(yeh-nehn pohr fah-bvohr ehl kooehs-teeoh-nah-reeoh)* (Please fill in the questions.)

✔ **Al llegar llévelo a la Aduana.** *(ahl yeh-gahr yeh-bveh-loh ah lah ah-dooah-nah)* (When you arrive, take it to Customs.)

If you're flying into a country, airport personnel can help you get to passport control. Here are some phrases that you may hear during this process:

✔ **Pase a Inmigración.** *(pah-seh a een-mee-grah-seeohn)* (Go to Immigration.)

✔ **Pase por aquí con su pasaporte en la mano.** *(pah-seh pohr ah-kee kohn soo pah-sah-pohr-teh ehn lah mah-noh)* (Go this way with your passport in your hand.)

No matter which way you enter the country, be ready to answer some of these questions:

✔ **¿De dónde viene?** *(deh dohn-deh bveeeh-neh)* (Where do you come from?)

✔ **¿En qué vuelo llegó?** *(ehn keh bvooeh-loh yeh-goh)* (What flight did you come on?)

✔ **¿A dónde va?** *(ah dohn-deh bvah)* (Where are you going?)

✔ **¿Cuánto tiempo quiere quedarse en el país?** *(kooahn-toh teeehm-poh keeeh-reh keh-dahr-seh* ehn ehl pah-_ees_) (How long do you want to stay in the country?)

✔ **¿Cuánto dinero trae consigo?** _(koo_ahn_-toh dee-_neh_-roh traheh kohn-_see_-goh)_ (How much money do you have with you?)

✔ **¡Que tenga una estadía feliz!** _(keh _tehn_-gah _oo_-nah ehs-tah-_dee_-ah feh-_lees_)_ (Have a happy stay!)

✔ **Pase a la Aduana, por favor.** _(_pah_-seh ahl lah ah-doo_ah_-nah pohr fah-_bvohr_)_ (Go to Customs, please.)

Words to Know

Inmigración	een-mee-grah-see-_ohn_	Immigration
el documento	ehl doh-koo-_mehn_-toh	the document; the paper
el pasaporte	ehl pah-sah-_pohr_-teh	the passport
quedar	keh-_dahr_	to stay
el dinero	ehl dee-_neh_-roh	the money
la estadía	lah ehs-tah-_dee_-ah	the stay

Here are some phrases to know when dealing with Customs:

✔ **¿Tiene algo que declarar?** _(teee_eh_-neh _ahl_-goh keh deh-klah-_rahr_)_ (Do you have anything to declare?)

✔ **No, no tengo nada que declarar.** _(noh noh _tehn_-goh _nah_-dah keh deh-klah-_rahr_)_ (No, I have nothing to declare.)

✔ **Necesitamos revisar sus maletas.** *(neh-seh-see-tah-mohs reh-bvee-sahr soos mah-leh-tahs)* (We need to see your suitcases.)

✔ **¿Este objeto paga derechos?** *(ehs-teh ohbv-Heh-toh pah-gah deh-reh-chohs)* (Does one pay duties on this item? [Literally: Does this object pay duties?])

✔ **¿Cuánto se paga en derechos por este objeto?** *(kooahn-toh se pah-gah ehn deh-reh-chohs pohr ehs-teh ohbv-Heh-toh)* (How much duties does one pay for this thing [object]?)

✔ **Debe pagar impuestos.** *(deh-bveh pah-gahr eem-pooehs-tohs)* (You have to pay duty.)

✔ **Está libre de impuestos.** *(ehs-tah lee-bvreh de eem-pooehs-tohs)* (It's duty free.)

✔ **¿Trae algún material explosivo?** *(trah-eh ahl-goon mah-teh-reeahl ehks-ploh-see-bvoh)* (Do you have anything explosive? [Literally: Do you bring?])

✔ **¿Trae alguna bebida alcohólica?** *(trah-eh ahl-goo-nah bveh-bvee-dah ahl-koh-oh-lee-kah)* (Do you have any alcoholic beverages?)

✔ **¿Trae algún aparato eléctrico?** *(trah-eh ahl-goon ah-pah-rah-toh eh-lehk-tree-koh)* (Do you have any electrical devices?)

✔ **Sólo para mi uso personal.** *(soh-loh pah-rah mee oo-soh pehr-soh-nahl)* (Only for my personal use.)

Here are some phrases that you may need to know when registering your electrical equipment:

✔ **Por favor llene este formulario.** *(pohr fah-bvohr yeh-neh ehs-teh foh-moo-lah-reeoh)* (Please fill in this form.)

✔ **¿Cuáles son las máquinas que hay que registrar?** *(kooah-lehs sohn lahs mah-kee-nahs keh ahy keh reh-Hees-trahr)* (Which electrical devices do we have to register?)

✔ **Al salir del país debe presentar este formulario.** *(ahl sah-leer dehl pahees deh-bveh preh-sehn-tahr ehs-teh fohr-moo-lah-reeoh)* (When you exit the country, you must show this form.)

✔ **Puede pasar hacia la salida.** *(pooeh-deh pah-sahr ah-seeah lah sah-lee-dah)* (You may proceed to the exit.)

Words to Know

la aduana	lah ah-dooah-nah	Customs
el aparato	ehl ah-pah-rah-toh	the machine; the appliance
uso personal	oo-soh pehr-soh-nahl	personal use
revisar	reh-bvee-sahr	to go through
las maletas	lahs mah-leh-tahs	the suitcases
abrir	ah-bvreer	to open
afeitar	ah-fehee-tahr	to shave
la cámara de video	lah kah-mah-rah deh bvee-dehoh	the video camera
la computadora portátil	lah kohm-poo-tah-doh-rah pohr-tah-teel	the laptop computer
salir	sah-leer	to exit; to get out

Transportation Verbs

When you go out on the town, you do a lot of "going out" — and a lot of waiting: waiting on buses, on taxis, on your friends. So here are a couple helpful verbs: **salir** (sah-_leer_) (to go out) and **esperar** (ehs-_pehr_-ahr) (to wait).

The outgoing verb: Salir

Salir (sah-_leer_) (to go out) is an irregular verb that has many different uses. Here are just a few of the uses of this outgoing verb:

- ✔ **¿De dónde sale el tranvía a Callao?** (deh _dohn_-deh _sah_-leh ehl trahn-_bveeah_ ah kah-_yah_-oh) (Where does the Callao street car leave from?)

- ✔ **¿Cada cuánto sale el bus?** (_kah_-dah koo_ahn_-toh _sah_-leh ehl bvoos) (How often does the bus leave?)

- ✔ **Salimos a andar en trolebús.** (sah-_lee_-mohs ah ahn-_dahr_ ehn troh-leh-_bvoos_) (We went out to ride around in the trolley bus.)

- ✔ **Ellos salen de la estación del tren.** (_eh_-yohs _sah_-lehn deh lah ehs-tah-seeohn dehl trehn) (They are going out of the station.)

- ✔ **Vamos a salir en la calle Oro.** (_bvah_-mohs ah sah-_leer_ ehn lah _kah_-yeh _oh_-roh) (We'll come out at Oro street.)

Here's how you conjugate **salir** in the present tense:

Conjugation	Pronunciation
yo salgo	yoh _sahl_-goh
tú sales	too _sah_-lehs
él, ella, ello, uno, usted sale	ehl, _eh_-yah, _eh_-yoh, _oo_-noh, oos-_tehd_, _sah_-leh
nosotros salimos	noh-_soh_-trohs sah-_lee_-mohs

Conjugation	Pronunciation
vosotros salís	bvoh-<u>soh</u>-trohs sah-<u>lees</u>
ellos, ellas, ustedes salen	<u>eh</u>-yohs, <u>eh</u>-yahs, oos-<u>teh</u>-dehs <u>sah</u>-lehn

Using the waiting verb: Esperar

Esperar *(ehs-pehr-<u>ahr</u>)* is the verb of hoping and waiting — maybe you're waiting because you're hoping. In any case, **esperar** is a regular verb, easy to handle, as shown in the following conjugation in the present tense. The root of this verb is **esper-** *(ehs-<u>pehr</u>)*; this is the part of the verb to which you add the various endings.

Conjugation	Pronunciation
yo espero	yoh ehs-<u>peh</u>-roh
tú esperas	too ehs-<u>peh</u>-rahs
él, ella, ello, uno, usted espera	ehl, <u>eh</u>-yah, <u>eh</u>-yoh, <u>oo</u>-noh, oos-<u>tehd</u>, ehs-<u>peh</u>-rah
nosotros esperamos	noh-<u>soh</u>-trohs ehs-peh-<u>rah</u>-mohs
vosotros esperáis	bvoh-<u>soh</u>-trohs ehs-peh-<u>rahees</u>
ellos, ellas, ustedes esperan	<u>eh</u>-yohs, <u>eh</u>-yahs, oos-<u>teh</u>-dehs ehs-<u>peh</u>-rahn

Esperar que *(ehs-peh-rahr keh)* is hoping. **Esperar** plain and simple is waiting. Here are some phrases you may use when you're waiting and hoping:

> ✔ **Espero que le guste mi auto.** *(ehs-<u>peh</u>-roh keh leh <u>goos</u>-teh mee <u>ahoo</u>-toh)* (I hope you'll like my car.)

> ✔ **Esperamos en la cola.** *(ehs-peh-<u>rah</u>-mohs ehn lah <u>koh</u>-lah)* (We are waiting in line.)

✔ **Espero que venga el taxi.** (ehs-_peh_-roh keh _bvehn_-gah ehl _tah_-ksee) (I hope the taxi will come.)

✔ **Espero el taxi.** (ehs-_peh_-roh ehl _tah_-ksee) (I'm waiting for the taxi.)

✔ **No esperamos más el bus.** (noh ehs-peh-_rah_-mohs mahs ehl bvoos) (We won't wait for the bus any longer.)

✔ **Deben esperar el avión.** (_deh_-bvehn ehs-peh-_rahr_ ehl ah-bvee_ohn_) (They must wait for the plane.)

✔ **Espera el camión de Insurgentes.** (ehs-_peh_-rah ehl kah-mee_ohn_ deh een-soor-_Hehn_-tehs) (He waits for the Insurgentes bus. [Mexico])

Asking for Directions

Getting around in a city can be fun but also confusing. Fortunately, many people are willing to give directions. Just ask, and you'll get answers. Most people love to help.

¿Adónde vamos? Where do we go?

¿Dónde? (dohn-deh) (where) is most often used with **estar** (ehs-tahr), the verb that means "to be" in a temporary state. Check out the following sentences that use **¿dónde?** and **estar:**

✔ **¿Dónde está el Museo de Larco?** (_donh_-deh ehs-_tah_ ehl moo-_seh_-oh deh _lahr_-koh) (Where is the Larco Museum?)

✔ **¿Dónde estamos ahora?** (_dohn_-deh ehs-_tah_-mohs ah-_oh_-rah) (Where are we now?)

✔ **¿Dónde está el Hotel del Camino?** (_dohn_-deh ehs-_tah_ ehl oh-_tehl_ dehl kah-_mee_-noh) (Where is the Hotel del Camino?)

✔ **¿Dónde estuviste anoche?** (_dohn_-deh ehs-too-_bvees_-teh ah-_noh_-cheh) (Where were you last night?)

Mapping the place

Maps are your keys to getting around. And nearly all maps are oriented to the following directions:

- ✔ **el norte** *(ehl nohr-teh)* (the north)

- ✔ **el sur** *(ehl soor)* (the south)

- ✔ **el este** *(ehl ehs-teh)* (the east)

- ✔ **el oriente** *(ehl oh-reeehn-teh)* (the east [Literally: where the sun originates])

- ✔ **el oeste** *(ehl oh-ehs-teh)* (the west)

- ✔ **el poniente** *(ehl poh-neeehn-teh)* (the west [Literally: where the sun sets])

Here are some mapping phrases that may help you out:

- ✔ **La avenida Venus está al este de aquí.** *(lah ah-bveh-nee-dah bveh-noos ehs-tah ahl ehs-teh deh ah-kee)* (Venus Avenue is east of here.)

- ✔ **Al oeste se encuentra la calle Las Violetas.** *(ahl oh-ehs-teh seh ehn-kooehn-trah lah kah-yeh lahs bveeoh-leh-tahs)* (To the west is Violetas street.)

- ✔ **El parque está al norte.** *(ehl pahr-keh ehs-tah ahl nohr-teh)* (The park is at the north.)

- ✔ **Al sur se va hacia el río.** *(ahl soor seh bvah ah-see-ah ehl reeoh)* (To the south, is [Literally: one goes toward] the river.)

The phrases in Table 9-1 are helpful when asking or giving general directions.

Table 9-1	Direction Words	
Spanish	*Pronunciation*	*English*
la calle	lah kah-yeh	the street
la avenida	lah ah-bveh-nee-dah	the avenue
el bulevar	ehl bvoo-leh-bvahr	the boulevard

(continued)

Table 9-1 *(continued)*

Spanish	Pronunciation	English
el río	ehl <u>ree</u>-oh	the river
la plaza	lah <u>plah</u>-sah	the square
el parque	ehl <u>pahr</u>-keh	the park
el jardín	ehl Hahr-<u>deen</u>	the garden; sometimes a small park
el barrio	ehl <u>bvah</u>-rreeoh	the neighborhood
izquierda	ees-keee<u>ehr</u>-dah	left
derecha	deh-<u>reh</u>-chah	right
derecho	deh-<u>reh</u>-choh	straight
cerca	<u>sehr</u>-kah	near; close
lejos	<u>leh</u>-Hohs	far
doblar	doh-<u>bvlahr</u>	to turn
seguir	seh-<u>gheer</u>	to keep going
la cuadra	lah koo<u>ah</u>-drah	the block
la manzana	lah mahn-<u>sah</u>-nah	the block

Getting directions from locals

Asking for directions is always a bit problematic. The people who answer your questions know the city, and the answers seem so obvious to them! So to keep you going and to sharpen your ear, here are some phrases you may be able to put to good use:

✔ **En el barrio hay una avenida ancha.** *(ehn ehl <u>bvah</u>-rreeoh ahy <u>oo</u>-nah ah-bveh-<u>nee</u>-dah <u>ahn</u>-chah)* (In the neighborhood, there is a wide avenue.)

✔ **Nuestra calle va de norte a sur.** *(nooe<u>ehs</u>-trah <u>kah</u>-yeh bvah deh <u>nohr</u>-teh ah soor)* (Our street runs north-south.)

✔ **Mi tía vive en la Cerrada del Olivo.** *(mee teeah bvee-bveh ehn lah seh-rrah-dah dehl oh-lee-bvoh)* (My aunt lives at the Cerrada [street with no exit] del Olivo [olive tree].)

✔ **Junto al río hay un gran parque.** *(Hoon-toh ahl reeoh ahy oon grahn pahr-keh)* (On the river side there is a large park.)

✔ **La plaza está en el centro de la ciudad.** *(lah plah-sah ehs-tah ehn ehl sehn-troh deh lah seeoo-dahd)* (The square is in the center of the city.)

✔ **En el jardín hay juegos para niños.** *(ehn ehl Hahr-deen ahy Hooeh-gohs pah-rah nee-nyohs)* (In the small park, they have a children's playground.)

✔ **El Zócalo de México es una plaza enorme.** *(ehl soh-kah-loh deh meh-Hee-koh ehs oo-nah plah-sah eh-nohr-meh)* (The Zocalo in Mexico is an immense square.)

✔ **Esa avenida se llama La Alameda.** *(eh-sah ah-bveh-nee-dah seh yah-mah lah ah-lah-meh-dah)* (The name of that avenue is La Alameda [Poplar Grove].)

Be prepared to listen to a long string of directions like this list:

✔ **Disculpe, ¿cómo llego al Museo de la Estampa?** *(dees-kool-peh koh-moh yeh-goh ahl moo-seh-oh deh lah ehs-tahm-pah)* (Excuse me, how do I get to the Graphics Museum?)

✔ **Muy fácil. Está muy cerca.** *(mooy fah-seel esh-tah mooy sehr-kah)* (Very easy. It's very close.)

Sale del hotel. *(sah-leh dehl oh-tehl)* (You go out of the hotel.)

Al salir va hacia la izquierda. *(ahl sah-leer bvah ah-seeah lah ees-keeehr-dah)* (As you get out, you go to the left)

camina hasta la segunda calle *(kah-mee-nah ahs-tah lah seh-goon-dah kah-yeh)* (walk to the second street)

> **da vuelta a la derecha, una cuadra** *(dah bvoo<u>ehl</u>-tah ah lah deh-<u>reh</u>-chah oo-nah koo<u>ah</u>-drah)* (turn to the right, go one block)
>
> **y llega al museo.** *(ee <u>yeh</u>-gah ahl moo-<u>seh</u>-oh)* (and you arrive at the museum.)

> ✔ **Subes por esa calle, a la izquierda.** *(<u>soo</u>-bvehs pohr eh-sah <u>kah</u>-yeh, ah lah ees-kee<u>ehr</u>-dah)* (You go up on that street, to the left.)

> ✔ **Bajamos por esta calle.** *(bvah-<u>Hah</u>-mohs pohr <u>ehs</u>-tah <u>kah</u>-yeh)* (We go down this street.)

Understanding spatial directions

We use words to tell where people or things are in relation to other people and things. You can use these terms to describe those relationships:

> ✔ **al lado** *(ahl <u>lah</u>-doh)* (beside, next to, at the side of)
>
> ✔ **al frente** *(ahl <u>frehn</u>-teh)* (in front of)
>
> ✔ **dentro** *(<u>dehn</u>-troh)* (inside)
>
> ✔ **adentro** *(ah-<u>dehn</u>-troh)* (inside; because **dentro** also means "inside," **adentro** may express movement, as when someone or something moves toward an interior)
>
> ✔ **fuera** *(foo<u>eh</u>-rah)* (outside)
>
> ✔ **afuera** *(ah-foo<u>eh</u>-rah)* (outside; can express movement, as in the case of **adentro**, earlier in this list)
>
> ✔ **bajo** *(<u>bvah</u>-Hoh)* (under; below)
>
> ✔ **debajo** *(deh-<u>bvah</u>-Hoh)* (underneath)
>
> ✔ **arriba** *(ah-<u>ree</u>-bvah)* (above)

Practicing these directions comes in handy. The sentences that follow use spatial-direction terms:

> ✔ **La pastelería está al lado del banco.** *(lah-pahs-teh-leh-<u>ree</u>ah ehs-<u>tah</u> ahl <u>lah</u>-doh dehl <u>bvahn</u>-koh)* (The pastry shop is next to the bank.)

✔ **Al frente del banco hay una zapatería.** *(ahl frehn-teh dehl bvahn-koh ahy oo-nah sah-pah-teh-reeah)* (In front of the bank there is a shoe store.)

✔ **Las mesas del café están afuera.** *(lahs meh-sahs dehl kah-feh ehs-tahn ah-fooeh-rah)* (The tables of the cafe are outside.)

✔ **Debajo de la calle corre el tren subterráneo.** *(deh-bvah-Hoh deh lah kah-yeh koh-rreh ehl trehn soobv-teh-rrah-neh-oh)* (The subway runs under the street.)

✔ **Este ascensor va arriba.** *(ehs-teh ah-sehn-sohr bvah ah-rree-bvah)* (This elevator goes up.)

Words to Know

encontrar	ehn-kohn-trahr	to find
la rama	lah rah-mah	the branch
la esquina	lah ehs-kee-nah	the corner
correr	koh-rrehr	to run
lejano	leh-Hah-noh	distant; far

Here, there, and everywhere

In Spanish, you can indicate here and there in two ways. Native Spanish speakers interchange *here* and *there* often, with no distinction between the two words. *Here* and *there* are adverbs; they always work in the vicinity of a verb and words that talk about space.

✔ **allá** *(ah-yah)* (there)

✔ **allí** *(ah-yee)* (there)

✔ **acá** *(ah-kah)* (here)

✔ **aquí** *(ah-kee)* (here)

To show that it makes no difference whether you use one of these pairs of words or the other, the following sentences enable you to practice situations in which you may use *here* or *there:*

- **Allí, en la esquina, está el banco.** *(ah-yee ehn lah ehs-kee-nah ehs-tah ehl bvan-koh)* (There, on the corner, is the bank.)

- **Allá van los turistas.** *(ah-yah bvahn lohs too-rees-tahs)* (There go the tourists.)

- **Aquí se come muy bien.** *(ah-kee seh koh-meh mooy bveehn)* (Here one eats very well.)

- **Acá está el museo.** *(ah-kah ehs-tah ehl moo-seh-oh)* (Here is the museum.)

- **¡Ven acá!** *(bvehn ah-kah)* (Come here!)

- **¡Corre allá!** *(koh-rreh ah-yah)* (Run there!)

You can use the following phrases to express the idea of all places or no particular places in Spanish:

- **en todas partes** *(ehn toh-dahs pahr-tehs)* (everywhere)

- **en ninguna parte** *(ehn neen-goo-nah pahr-teh)* (nowhere, anywhere)

Chapter 10

Laying Down Your Weary Head: House or Hotel?

....

In This Chapter

▶ Checking out the amenities

▶ Registering for your room

▶ Using the verbs for sleeping and waking

....

*W*hether you've been working at the office, shopping, or traveling, at the end of the day, you need a place to lay your head. This chapter gives you the phrases you need to find a house or a hotel.

Speaking of Houses . . .

La casa *(lah kah-sah)* (the house): These words express in Spanish what you call home in English. La casa can also express the building in which you make your home.

The Spanish word **el hogar** *(ehl oh-gahr)* (the home) is closest in meaning to "the hearth" in English. **El hogar** invokes the fire in a shelter where warmth and food are offered. **El hogar** is a place of warmth during the cold days, a place to stay dry during rain and snow, a place of repose when you're tired, a place of joy during the many happy events of your life.

Use the following phrases to discuss your house and home:

- ✔ **Hogar dulce hogar.** *(oh-_gahr_ _dool_-seh oh-_gahr_)* (Home sweet home.)

- ✔ **Especialidad de la casa.** *(ehs-peh-seeah-lee-_dahd_ deh lah _kah_-sah)* (Specialty of the house.)

- ✔ **Un error grande como una casa.** *(oon eh-_rrohr_ _grahn_-deh _koh_-moh _oo_-nah _kah_-sah)* (An immense mistake. [Literally: A mistake the size of a house.])

- ✔ **Anda como Pedro por su casa.** *(_ahn_-dah _koh_-moh _peh_-droh pohr soo _kah_-sah)* (Acts like he owns the place. [Literally: Goes about like Pedro in his house.])

- ✔ **Mudarse de casa.** *(moo-_dahr_-seh deh _kah_-sah)* (To move. [Literally: To change houses.])

Some rental wisdom

More likely than not, you're going to begin living on your own in a rented property, which can include several different kinds of housing. Use the following phrases to help you with your search:

- ✔ **edificio de apartamentos** *(eh-dee-_fee_-seeoh deh ah-pahr-tah-_mehn_-tohs)* (apartment building)

- ✔ **casa de una planta** *(_kah_-sah deh _oo_-nah _plahn_-tah)* (one-story house)

- ✔ **casa de dos pisos** *(_kah_-sah deh dohs _pee_-sohs)* (two-story house)

- ✔ **casa adosada** *(_kah_-sah ah-doh-_sah_-dah)* (semi-detached house [meaning one of its walls touches the wall of the neighboring house])

- ✔ **casa residencial** *(_kah_-sah reh-see-dehn-see_ahl_)* (residence; house used for residential purposes)

- ✔ **apartamento en arriendo** *(ah-pahr-tah-_mehn_-toh ehn ah-rree_ehn_-doh)* (apartment for rent)

✔ **apartamento en régimen de propiedad hori-**
zontal *(ah-pahr-tah-mehn-toh ehn reh-Hee-mehn*
deh proh-peeeh-dahd oh-ree-sohn-tahl) (condo-
minium) Literally, this phrase means an apartment that is governed by a set of rules related
to horizontal — meaning on the ground — real
estate.

Want to find out whether an apartment is available?
Try these phrases:

✔ **Vimos su aviso en el diario y llamamos por el**
apartamento. *(bvee-mohs soo ah-bvee-soh ehn*
ehl deeah-reeoh ee yah-mah-mos pohr ehl ah-pahr-
tah-mehn-toh) (We saw your ad in the paper, and
we're calling about the apartment.)

✔ **Busco un apartamento amueblado.** *(bvoos-koh*
oon-ah-pahr-tah-mehn-toh ah-mooeh-bvlah-doh)
(I'm looking for a furnished apartment.)

✔ **¿Está disponible?** *(ehs-tah dees-poh-nee-bvleh)*
(Is it available?)

✔ **Les recomiendo ese otro apartamento.** *(lehs*
reh-koh-meeehn-doh eh-seh oh-tro ah-pahr-tah-
mehn-toh) (I recommend the other apartment.)

✔ **¿Cuándo podemos verlo?** *(kooahn-doh poh-deh-*
mohs bvehr-loh) (When can we see it?)

✔ **Mañana en la tarde se desocupa.** *(mah-nyah-*
nah ehn lah tahr-deh seh dehs-oh-koo-pah) (It will
be vacant tomorrow afternoon.)

✔ **Venimos a ver el apartamento.** *(bveh-nee-mohs*
ah bvehr ehl ah-pahr-tah-mehn-toh) (We came to
see the apartment.)

Once you're at the apartment, here are some questions you may want to ask:

✔ **Esta casa ¿cuántos baños tiene?** *(ehs-tah kah-*
sah kooahn-tohs bvah-nyohs teeeh-neh) (How
many bathrooms does this house have?)

✔ **¿Dónde está la cocina?** *(dohn-deh ehs-tah lah*
koh-see-nah) (Where's the kitchen?)

✔ **¿Hay cocina a gas o eléctrica?** *(ahy koh-see-nah ah gahs oh eh-lehk-tree-kah)* (Is there a gas or electric stove?)

✔ **¿Cuántas habitaciones hay?** *(kooahn-tahs ah-bvee-tah-seeoh-nehs ahy)* (How many rooms are there?)

✔ **¿El gas y el agua están incluídos en el arriendo?** *(ehl gahs ee ehl ah-gooah ehs-tahn een-klooee-dohs ehn ehl ah-rreeehn-doh)* (Are gas and water included in the rent?)

✔ **¿Se necesita hacer un depósito?** *(Se neh-seh-see-tah ah-sehr oon deh-poh-see-toh)* (Do we have to give you a down payment?)

✔ **Vamos a pensarlo, mañana volvemos.** *(bvah-mohs ah pehn-sahr-loh mah-nyah-nah bvohl-bveh-mohs)* (We're going to think about it. We'll come back tomorrow.)

Words to Know

disponible	dees-poh-nee-bvleh	available
ocupar	oh-koo-pahr	to take up; to occupy
desocupar	dehs-oh-koo-pahr	to vacate
lástima	lahs-tee-mah	pity; shame
el depósito	ehl deh-poh-see-toh	the deposit
reembolsar	reh-ehm-bvol-sahr	to refund
incluido	een-klooee-doh	included
pagar	pah-gahr	to pay
amueblado	ah-mooeh-bvlah-doh	furnished
limpiar	leèm-pee-ahr	to clean

Furnishing your house

Once you've found an apartment, you'll need furnish the rooms. The words in Table10-1 will help you out:

Table 10-1	Around the House	
Spanish	*Pronunciation*	*Translation*
la habitación	lah ah-bvee-tah-see<u>ohn</u>	the room
el cuarto	ehl koo<u>ah</u>r-toh	the room
la cocina	lah koh-<u>see</u>-nah	the kitchen
el refrigerador	ehl reh-free-Heh-rah-<u>dohr</u>	the refrigerator
la estufa	lah ehs-<u>too</u>-fah	the stove (in Mexico)
la microondas	mee-kroh-<u>ohn</u>-dahs	microwave
el comedor	ehl koh-meh-<u>dohr</u>	the dining room
la sala	lah <u>sah</u>-lah	the living room
el living	ehl <u>lee</u>-bveeng	the living room (in Chile)
el sillón	ehl see-<u>yohn</u>	armchair
el reloj (pared)	ehl reh-<u>loH</u>	clock
la sofá	lah soh-<u>fah</u>	sofa
el televisor	ehl teh-leh-bvee-<u>sohr</u>	television
los baños	lohs <u>bvah</u>-nyohs	the bathrooms
medio baño	<u>meh</u>-deeoh <u>bvah</u>-nyoh	half-bathroom (a bathroom with no shower or tub)
la bañera	lah bah-<u>nyeh</u>-rah	bath

(continued)

Table 10-1 *(continued)*

Spanish	Pronunciation	Translation
el espejo	ehl es-<u>peh</u>-Hoh	mirror
la ducha	lah <u>doo</u>-chah	shower
el lavabo	ehl lah-<u>bvah</u>-bvoh	sink
el dormitorio	ehl dohr-mee-<u>toh</u>-reeoh	the bedroom (in Chile and Argentina)
la recámara	lah reh-<u>kah</u>-mah-rah	the bedroom (in Mexico)
la cama	lah <u>kah</u>-mah	bed
la manta	lah <u>mahn</u>-ta	blanket
la almohada	lah ahl-moh-<u>ah</u>-dah	pillow
la lámpara	lah <u>lahm</u>-pah-rah	lamp
la alfombra	lah ahl-<u>fohm</u>-brah	rug
la estantería	lah es-tan-teh-<u>ree</u>-ah	shelves
el armario	ehl ahr-<u>mahr</u>-eeoh	wardrobe
el secador	ehl seh-kah-<u>dor</u>	dryer
la lavadora	lah lah-bvah-<u>doh</u>-rah	washing machine
el aspirador	ehl ah-spee-rah-<u>dohr</u>	vacuum cleaner

Scoping Out the Hotel

By the time you get to your hotel, you're probably tired from your travels. However, even as tired as you are, you probably want to see the rooms before you check in.

Knowing the following phrases before you arrive at your hotel can make getting a room much easier.

- ✔ **con baño** *(kohn bvah-nyoh)* (with bathroom)

- ✔ **con agua caliente** *(kohn ah-gooah kah-leeehn-teh)* (with hot water)

- ✔ **sólo con agua fría** *(soh-loh kohn ah-gooah free-ah)* (with cold water only)

- ✔ **a la calle** *(ah lah kah-yeh)* (opening to the street)

- ✔ **al interior** *(ahl een-teh-reeohr)* (opening to the interior)

- ✔ **estacionamiento** *(ehs-tah-seeoh-nah-mee-ehn-toh)* (parking)

- ✔ **la piscina** *(lah pee-see-nah)* (the swimming pool) — in Mexico, use **la alberca** *(lah ahl-bvehr-kah)* instead

Words to Know

la cuadra	lah koo-ah-drah	the block
el portón	ehl pohr-tohn	the [large] door; doorway
abrir	ah-bvreer	to open
esperar	ehs-peh-rahr	to wait

When you're ready to get the room, these phrases help you out:

- ✔ **Necesito una habitación, con baño.** *(neh-seh-see-toh oo-nah ah-bvee-tah-seeohn kohn bvah-nyoh)* (I need a room, with bathroom.)

- ✔ **¿Le gusta hacia la calle o hacia el patio?** *(leh goos-tah ah-seeah lah kah-yeh oh ah-seeah ehl pah-teeoh)* (Do you prefer a room facing the street or the patio?)

✔ **Las del patio son muy tranquilas.** *(lahs dehl <u>pah</u>-teeoh sohn mooy trahn-<u>kee</u>-lahs)* (The patio rooms are very quiet.)

✔ **Las habitaciones hacia el patio cuestan cuarenta pesos, sin desayuno.** *(lahs ah-bvee-tah-see<u>oh</u>-nehs <u>ah</u>-seeah ehl <u>pah</u>-teeoh kooo<u>ehs</u>-tahn kooah-<u>rehn</u>-tah <u>peh</u>-sohs seen deh-sah-<u>yoo</u>-noh)* (The rooms facing the patio cost forty pesos, without breakfast.)

✔ **Prefiero una en el primer piso.** *(preh-fee<u>eh</u>-roh <u>oo</u>-nah ehn ehl pree-<u>mehr</u> <u>pee</u>-soh)* (I prefer one on the first floor.)

✔ **¿Prefiere con cama matrimonial o con dos camas?** *(preh-fee<u>eh</u>-reh kohn <u>kah</u>-mah mah-tree-moh-nee<u>ahl</u> oh kohn dohs <u>kah</u>-mahs)* (Do you prefer a double bed or two beds?)

✔ **Tengo disponible en el primer piso la habitación número ciento diecinueve. ¿Quiere verla?** *(<u>tehn</u>-goh dees-poh-<u>nee</u>-bvleh ehn ehl pree-<u>mehr</u> <u>pee</u>-soh lah ah-bvee-tah-see<u>ohn</u> <u>noo</u>-meh-roh <u>seeehn</u>-toh-dee<u>eeh</u>-see-noo<u>eh</u>-bveh kee<u>eh</u>-reh <u>bvehr</u>-lah)* (Room 119 is available on the first floor. Do you want to see it?)

✔ **Sí, quiero verla.** *(see kee<u>eh</u>-roh <u>bvehr</u>-lah)* (Yes, I want to see it.)

✔ **Aquí está la llave.** *(ah-<u>kee</u> ehs-<u>tah</u> lah <u>yah</u>-bveh)* (Here's the key.)

Words to Know

la cama	lah <u>kah</u>-mah	the bed
matrimonial	mah-tree-moh-nee-<u>ahl</u>	double (Literally: for married people)

ver	bvehr	to see
acompañar	ah-kohm-pah-<u>nyahr</u>	to go with; to accompany
preferir	preh-feh-<u>reer</u>	to prefer
la llave	lah <u>yah</u>-bveh	the key

If you want to relax in your room, you may want to check a few other things out:

- ✔ **¿Tiene baño?** *(tee-<u>eh</u>-neh <u>bvah</u>-nyoh)* (Does it have a [private] bathroom?)

- ✔ **¿El baño tiene tina?** *(ehl <u>bvah</u>-nyoh tee<u>eh</u>-neh <u>tee</u>-nah)* (Does the bathroom have a bathtub?)

- ✔ **¿La habitación tiene televisión?** *(lah ah-bvee-tah-see<u>ohn</u> tee<u>eh</u>-neh teh-leh-bvee-see<u>ohn</u>)* (Does the room have TV?)

- ✔ **¿Se puede ver canales en inglés?** *(seh poo<u>eh</u>-deh bvehr kah-<u>nah</u>-lehs ehn een-<u>glehs</u>)* (Can you get channels in English?)

Words to Know

la tina	lah <u>tee</u>-nah	the tub
ducharse	doo-<u>chahr</u>-seh	to take a shower
la ventana	lah bvehn-<u>tah</u>-nah	the window
abrir	ah-<u>bvreer</u>	to open
el mueble	ehl moo-<u>eh</u>-bvleh	the cabinet
el canal	ehl kah-<u>nahl</u>	the channel

Registering for a Room

If you're satisfied with the room, you're ready to register:

- ✔ **Me gusta la habitación ciento diecinueve. La voy a tomar.** *(meh goos-tah lah ah-bvee-tah-seeohn seeehn-toh deeeh-see-nooeh-bveh lah bvohy ah toh-mahr)* (I like the room. I'm going to take it.)

- ✔ **¿Cuántos días desea quedarse?** *(koo-ahn-tohs deeahs deh-seh-ah keh-dahr-seh)* (How many days do you want to stay?)

- ✔ **El desayuno no está incluído en el precio.** *(ehl deh-sah-yoo-noh noh ehs-tah een-klooee-doh ehn ehl preh-seeoh)* (Breakfast is not included in the price.)

- ✔ **¿Va a hacer un depósito por la primera noche?** *(bvah ah ah-sehr oon deh-poh-see-toh pohr lah pree-meh-rah noh-cheh)* (Are you going to make a deposit for the first night?)

- ✔ **Sí, lo voy a hacer. ¿Con tarjeta o efectivo?** *(see loh bvohy ah ah-sehr kohn tahr-Heh-tah oh eh-fehk-tee-bvoh)* (Yes, I'll make it. Cash or credit card?)

- ✔ **¿Me pueden despertar a las siete de la mañana?** *(meh pooeh-dehn dehs-pehr-tahr ah lahs seeeh-teh deh lah mah-nyah-nah)* (Can you wake me at seven in the morning?)

Words to Know

cuánto	koo-ahn-toh	how much
quedarse	keh-dahr-seh	to stay
registrarse	reh-Hees-trahr-seh	to check in
incluído	een-kloo-ee-doh	included
precio	ehl preh-seeoh	the price

Here are some terms to know when filling out your hotel registration form:

- **dirección permanente** *(dee-rehk-see-ohn pehr-mah-nehn-teh)* (permanent address)

- **calle, ciudad, estado, o provincia** *(kah-yeh seeoo-dahd ehs-tah-doh oh proh-bveen-seeah)* (street, city, state, or province)

- **país, código postal, teléfono** *(pahees koh-dee-goh pohs-tahl teh-leh-foh-noh)* (country, postal code, telephone)

- **número de su pasaporte** *(noo-meh-roh deh soo pah-sah-pohr-teh)* (your passport number)

- **si viene con vehículo . . .** *(see bveeeh-neh kohn bvehee-koo-loh)* If coming by vehicle . . .

- **número de placa de matrícula** *(noo-meh-roh deh plah-kah deh mah-tree-koo-lah)* (plate number)

- **fecha en que vence** *(feh-chah ehn keh bvehn-seh)* (expiration date)

Words to Know

llenar	yeh-nahr	to fill in
la ciudad	lah seeoo-dahd	the city
el estado	ehl ehs-tah-doh	the state
la provincia	lah proh-bveen-seeah	the province
el código postal	ehl koh-dee-goh pohs-tahl	the postal code [ZIP code]
el vehículo	ehl bveh-ee-koo-loh	the vehicle
la placa	lah plah-kah	the license plate
vencer	bvehn-sehr	to expire

When you visit any foreign country, always ask whether the water is safe to drink. You can never take the safety of your water for granted. Here are some phrases that help you determine how safe the water is:

- **¿Es potable el agua del hotel?** *(ehs poh-tah-bleh ehl ah-gooah dehl oh-tehl)* (Is the hotel's water drinkable?)

- **Sí, y también tenemos agua embotellada.** *(see ee tahm-bveeehn teh-neh-mohs ah-gooah ehm-bvoh-teh-yah-dah)* (Yes, and we also have bottled water.)

- **¿Dónde encuentro el agua?** *(dohn-deh ehn-kooehn-troh ehl ah-gooah)* (Where do I find the water?)

- **Las botellas están en su habitación.** *(lahs bvoh-teh-yahs ehs-tahn ehn soo ah-bvee-tah-seeohn)* (The bottles are in your room.)

Words to Know

la tarjeta	lah tahr-Heh-tah	the card
el efectivo	ehl eh-fehk-tee-bvoh	cash
la maleta	lah mah-leh-tah	the luggage; the suitcase
potable	poh-tah-bvleh	drinkable
embotellada	ehm-bvoh-teh-yah-dah	bottled
despertar	dehs-pehr-tahr	to awaken

As you finish checking in and settle into your room, some of these phrases may be helpful. (See Chapter 2 for more on possessive pronouns):

✔ **Esta es mi habitación.** *(ehs-tah ehs mee ah-bvee-tah-seeohn)* (This is my room.)

✔ **Tus llaves están en la mesa.** *(toos yah-bvehs ehs-tahn ehn lah meh-sah)* (Your keys are on the table.)

✔ **Sus llaves se las llevó la camarera.** *(soos yah-bvehs seh lahs yeh-bvoh lah kah-mah-reh-rah)* (The maid took his keys.)

✔ **Ese es nuestro hotel.** *(eh-seh ehs nooehs-troh oh-tehl)* (That is our hotel.)

✔ **Vinieron en su auto.** *(bvee-neeeh-rohn ehn soo ahoo-toh)* (They came in their car.)

✔ **Tus toallas están secas.** *(toos toh-ah-yahs ehs-tahn seh-kahs)* (Your towels are dry.)

✔ **Esas son mis maletas.** *(eh-sahs sohn mees mah-leh-tahs)* (Those are my suitcases.)

✔ **Nuestras sábanas están limpias.** *(nooehs-trahs sah-bvah-nahs ehs-tahn leem-peeahs)* (Our sheets are clean.)

✔ **Tu pasaporte está en la recepción.** *(too pah-sah-pohr-teh ehs-tah ehn lah reh-sehp-seeohn)* (Your passport is at the reception [desk].)

✔ **La cama esa es mía.** *(lah kah-mah eh-sah ehs meeah)* (That bed is mine.)

✔ **Esa maleta es la tuya.** *(eh-sah mah-leh-tah ehs lah too-yah)* (That suitcase is yours.)

✔ **La maleta que es tuya está en la recepción.** *(lah mah-leh-tah keh ehs too-yah ehs-tah ehn lah reh-sehp-seeohn)* (Your suitcase is at the reception desk.)

Dormir: The Sleeping Verb

After a long day, the sweet hour when you can finally rest and go to sleep comes. In Spanish, **dormir** *(dohr-meer)* (to sleep) is a bit irregular, much like a really tired person. See Table 10-2 for the conjugation.

Table 10-2	Dormir
Conjugation	*Pronunciation*
yo duermo	yoh doo-<u>ehr</u>-moh
tú duermes	too doo-<u>ehr</u>-mehs
él, ella, ello, uno, usted duerme	ehl <u>eh</u>-yah <u>eh</u>-yoh <u>oo</u>-noh oos-<u>tehd</u> doo-<u>ehr</u>-meh
nosotros dormimos	noh-<u>soh</u>-trohs dohr-<u>mee</u>-mohs
vosotros dormís	bvoh-<u>soh</u>-trohs dohr-<u>mees</u>
ellos, ellas, ustedes duermen	<u>eh</u>-yohs <u>eh</u>-yahs oos-<u>teh</u>-dehs doo-<u>ehr</u>-mehn

Here are some phrases to help you practice using **dormir:**

- ✔ **Yo duermo todos los días ocho horas.** *(yoh doo-<u>ehr</u>-moh <u>toh</u>-dohs lohs <u>dee</u>ahs <u>oh</u>-choh <u>oh</u>-rahs)* (I sleep eight hours every day.)

- ✔ **Camilo duerme en su cama.** *(kah-<u>mee</u>-loh doo-<u>ehr</u>-meh ehn soo <u>kah</u>-mah)* (Camilo sleeps in his bed.)

- ✔ **Dormimos en nuestra casa.** *(dohr-<u>mee</u>-mohs ehn noo<u>ehs</u>-trah <u>kah</u>-sah)* (We sleep in our home.)

- ✔ **Los invitados duermen en tu recámara.** *(lohs een-bvee-<u>tah</u>-dohs doo-<u>ehr</u>-mehn ehn too reh-<u>kah</u>-mah-rah)* (The guests sleep in your bedroom. [Mexico])

- ✔ **En mi cama duermen dos gatos.** *(ehn mee <u>kah</u>-mah doo-<u>ehr</u>-mehn dohs <u>gah</u>-tohs)* (Two cats sleep in my bed.)

- ✔ **Tú duermes con un osito.** *(too doo-<u>ehr</u>-mehs kohn oon oh-<u>see</u>-toh)* (You sleep with a little [teddy] bear.)

✔ **Los pájaros también duermen.** *(lohs pah-Hah-rohs tahm-bveeehn doo-ehr-mehn)* (The birds also sleep.)

Despertar: The Waking Up Verb

You use the verb **despertar** *(dehs-pehr-tahr)* (to awaken) after a good night's sleep. You can tell that this verb is irregular when you see that the root of the verb in the first person singular is different from that of the first person plural. See Table 10-3 for the conjugation of **despertar.**

Table 10-3	Despertar
Conjugation	*Pronunciation*
yo despierto	yoh dehs-peeehr-toh
tú despiertas	too dehs-peeehr-tahs
él, ella, ello, uno, usted despierta	ehl eh-yah eh-yoh oo-noh oos-tehd dehs-peeehr-tah
nosotros despertamos	noh-soh-trohs dehs-pehr-tah-mohs
vosotros despertáis	bvoh-soh-trohs dehs-pehr-tahees
ellos, ellas, ustedes despiertan	eh-yohs eh-yahs oos-teh-dehs dehs-peeehr-tahn

The following examples show you how to start practicing this verb:

✔ **Yo despierto temprano en la mañana.** *(yoh dehs-peeehr-toh tehm-prah-noh ehn lah mah-nyah-nah)* (I wake up early in the morning.)

✔ **Ustedes despiertan juntos.** *(oos-teh-dehs dehs-peeehr-tahn Hoon-tohs)* (You [formal] wake up together.)

✔ **Ellos no despiertan de noche.** *(<u>eh</u>-yohs noh dehs-pee<u>ehr</u>-tahn deh <u>noh</u>-cheh)* (They don't wake up at night.)

✔ **Despierta con el canto de los pájaros.** *(dehs-pee<u>ehr</u>-tah kohn ehl <u>kahn</u>-toh deh lohs <u>pah</u>-Hah-rohs)* (He awakens with the birds' singing.)

Chapter 11

Dealing with Emergencies

- -

In This Chapter

▶ Asking for help

▶ Talking about health problems

▶ Dealing with the police

▶ Getting help with car trouble

- -

*Y*ou should always be prepared for emergencies, especially in areas whose residents don't speak your native language. This chapter looks at two main areas where you may experience an emergency: health concerns — breaking an arm or experiencing stomach flu — and "legal" emergencies — car accidents and other law infractions that may require the help of your consulate or a lawyer.

Shouting for Help

You may find yourself in a situation where you need to cry for help. You probably don't have time to thumb through your dictionary, so you may want to memorize these words. You can use the first two interchangeably.

The following list gives you some basic distress-signaling words:

- ✔ **¡Socorro!** *(soh-koh-rroh)* (Help!)
- ✔ **¡Auxilio!** *(ahoo-ksee-leeoh)* (Help!)
- ✔ **¡Ayúdeme!** *(ah-yoo-deh-meh)* (Help me!)
- ✔ **¡Incendio!** *(een-sehn-deeoh)* (Fire!)
- ✔ **¡Inundación!** *(ee-noon-dah-seeohn)* (Flood!)
- ✔ **¡Temblor!** *(tehm-bvlohr)* (Earth tremor!)
- ✔ **¡Terremoto!** *(teh-rreh-moh-toh)* (Earthquake!)
- ✔ **¡Maremoto!** *(mah-reh-moh-toh)* (Tidal wave!)

You can help speed up your request by using one of these two words:

- ✔ **¡Rápido!** *(rah-pee-doh)* (Quick!)
- ✔ **¡Apúrense!** *(ah-poo-rehn-seh)* (Hurry!)

Handling Health Problems

Here are some sentences to help you be just as caring and kind, but at the same time firm with your refusal for help, when you don't want any. Suppose that the person trying to be helpful says things like

- ✔ **¡Pobrecito!, ¿le ayudo?** *(poh-bvreh-see-toh leh ah-yoo-doh)* (Poor little you [male], can I help you?)
- ✔ **¡Vengan todos, a ayudar!** *(bvehn-gahn toh-dohs ah ah-yoo-dar)* (Come, everybody, let's help him!)

In which case, you can answer with things like

- ✔ **Por favor, estoy bien, no me ayude.** *(pohr fah-bvohr ehs-tohy bveeen noh meh ah-yoo-deh)* (Please, I'm fine, don't help me.)

✔ **Muchas gracias, le agradezco, prefiero estar solo.** *(moo-chahs grah-seeahs leh ah-grah-dehs-koh preh-feeeh-roh ehs-tahr soh-loh)* (Thank you very much, I prefer to be alone.)

✔ **Estoy muy bien, gracias, no necesito ayuda.** *(ehs-tohy mooy bveeehn grah-seeahs noh neh-seh-see-toh ah-yoo-dah)* (I'm fine, thanks, I don't need help.)

✔ **Usted es muy gentil, gracias, no me ayude, por favor.** *(oos-tehd ehs mooy Hehn-teel grah-seeahs noh meh ah-yoo-deh pohr fah-bvohr)* (You're very kind, thanks, don't help me, please.)

✔ **Ustedes son muy amables, pero estoy bien.** *(oos-teh-dehs sohn mooy ah-mah-bvlehs peh-roh ehs-tohy bveeehn)* (You [formal, plural] are very kind, but I'm fine.)

Helping out

This section covers some phrases that you can use when you want to be formally helpful. The formal way of speech is more normal to use both on your part and on the part of those who are helping you. It shows respect on your part to the doctor, for example, and on his part to you. Neither of you have an intimate or informal relationship:

✔ **¿Le ayudo?** *(leh ah-yoo-doh)* (Can I help you?)

✔ **Sí, ayúdame a pedir una ambulancia.** *(see ah-yoo-deh-meh ah peh-deer oo-nah ahm-bvoo-lahn-seeah)* (Yes, help me get an ambulance.)

✔ **Espere. Le van a ayudar a cargar al herido.** *(ehs-peh-reh leh bvahn ah ah-yoo-dahr ah kahr-gahr ahl eh-ree-doh)* (Wait. They'll help you carry the injured person.)

✔ **Usted ayude al enfermo a bajar de la camilla.** *(oos-tehd ah-yoo-deh ahl ehn-fehr-moh ah bvah-Hahr deh lah kah-mee-yah)* (You go help the sick person get off the stretcher.)

✔ **¡Apúrese!** *(ah-poo-reh-seh)* (Hurry up!)

Words to Know

el enfermo	ehl ehn-_fehr_-moh	the sick person, male
la enferma	lah ehn-_fehr_-mah	the sick person, female
la camilla	lah kah-_mee_-yah	the stretcher; the trolley; the gurney
ayudar	ah-yoo-_dahr_	to help
cargar	kahr-_gahr_	to carry

The following phrases are for informal situations — if you're talking to a child or if the person helping you is someone that you know:

- ✔ **¿Te ayudo?** _(teh ah-yoo-doh)_ (Can I help you?)

- ✔ **Sí, ayúdame.** _(see ah-yoo-dah-meh)_ (Yes, help me.)

- ✔ **Te busco un médico.** _(teh bvoos-koh oon meh-dee-koh)_ (I'll get a doctor for you.)

- ✔ **¡Apúrate!** _(ah-poo-rah-teh)_ (Hurry up!)

- ✔ **¡Sujétame!** _(soo-Heh-tah-meh)_ (Hold onto me!)

Painful phrases for when it hurts

When you're hurt, you want to be able to tell people about it so that they can help ease your pain. The following sentences tell you how to talk about pain:

- ✔ **Me duele la espalda.** _(meh dooeh-leh lah ehs-pahl-dah)_ (My back hurts.)

- ✔ **¿Le duele la cabeza?** _(leh dooeh-leh lah kah-bveh-sah)_ (Does your head hurt? [single, formal])

✔ **Les duele todo.** *(lehs dooeh-leh toh-doh)* (They hurt all over.)

✔ **Nos duelen las manos.** *(nohs dooeh-lehn lahs mah-nohs)* (Our hands hurt.)

✔ **¿Te duele aquí?** *(teh dooeh-leh ah-kee)* (Does it hurt you [singular, informal] here?)

Words to Know

el médico	ehl meh-dee-koh	the doctor
la pierna	lah peeehr-nah	the leg
la fractura	lah frahk-too-rah	the fracture (medical term for broken bone)
la radiografía	lah rah-deeoh-grah-feeah	the X ray picture
el yeso	ehl yeh-soh	the plaster (either in casts or walls)
enyesar	ehn-yeh-sahr	to set in a cast
el analgésico	ehl ah-nahl-geh-see-koh	the pain killer

Getting help for a bleeding wound

The following list gives you some examples of how to get medical help for someone who's bleeding:

✔ **¡Hay una emergencia!** *(ahy oo-nah eh-mehr-Hehn-see-ah)* (There's an emergency!)

✔ **¡Traigan un médico!** (*trahee-gahn* oon *meh-dee-koh*) (Bring a doctor!)

✔ **¡Traigan una ambulancia!** (*trahee-gahn* oo-nah ahm-bvoo-*lahn*-seeah) (Bring an ambulance!)

✔ **Lo más rápido posible.** (*loh mahs rah-pee-doh poh-see-bleh*) (As fast as possible.)

✔ **Tiene un corte.** (*teeeh-neh oon kohr-teh*) (You [formal] have a cut.)

✔ **Necesita puntos.** (*neh-seh-see-tah poon-tohs*) (You [formal] need stitches.)

Words to Know

la *cabeza*	lah kah-bveh-sah	the head
la *emergencia*	lah eh-mehr-Hehn-seeah	the emergency
el *corte*	ehl kohr-teh	the cut
los *puntos*	lohs poon-tohs	the stitches [surgical]

Telling where it hurts

In this section, we give you several phrases that may be useful in telling someone where you hurt:

✔ **Me sangra la nariz.** (*meh sahn-grah lah nah-rees*) (My nose is bleeding.)

✔ **No puedo ver.** (*noh pooeh-doh bvehr*) (I can't see.)

✔ **Me entró algo en el ojo.** (*meh ehn-troh ahl-goh ehn ehl oh-Hoh*) (Something got into my eye.)

✔ **Me torcí el tobillo.** (*meh tohr-see ehl toh-bvee-yoh*) (I twisted my ankle.)

✔ **Se quebró el brazo derecho.** *(seh keh-broh ehl bvrah-soh deh-reh-choh)* (He broke his right arm.)

✔ **La herida está en el antebrazo.** *(lah eh-ree-dah ehs-tah ehn ehl ahn-teh-bvrah-soh)* (The wound is on the forearm.)

✔ **Le duele la muñeca izquierda.** *(leh dooeh-leh lah moo-nyeh-kah ees-keeehr-dah)* (Her left wrist hurts.)

✔ **Se cortó el dedo índice.** *(seh kohr-toh ehl deh-doh een-dee-seh)* (He cut his index finger.)

✔ **Se torció el cuello.** *(seh tohr-seeoh ehl kooeh-yoh)* (She twisted her neck.)

✔ **He sentido náuseas.** *(eh sehn-tee-doh nahoo-seh-ahs)* (I felt nauseated.)

Describing symptoms

Table 11-1 lists common terms for body parts that you may need to know when visiting the doctor.

Table 11-1	Helpful Words in a Medical Emergency	
Spanish	*Pronunciation*	*English*
Head and Neck Words		
el ojo	ehl oh-Hoh	the eye
la boca	lah bvoh-kah	the mouth
la lengua	lah lehn-gooah	the tongue
la oreja	lah oh-reh-Hah	the ear
la nariz	lah nah-rees	the nose
el rostro	ehl rohs-troh	the face
la barba	lah bvahr-bvah	the beard

(continued)

Table 11-1 *(continued)*

Spanish	Pronunciation	English
Head and Neck Words		
el bigote	el bvee-<u>goh</u>-teh	the whiskers; moustache
el cuello	ehl koo<u>eh</u>-yoh	the neck
las amígdalas	lahs ah-<u>meeg</u>-dah-lahs	the tonsils
Torso Words		
el hombro	ehl <u>ohm</u>-broh	the shoulder
el corazón	ehl koh-rah-<u>sohn</u>	the heart
el pulmón	el pool-<u>mohn</u>	the lung
el estómago	ehl ehs-<u>toh</u>-mah-goh	the stomach
el intestino	ehl een-tehs-<u>tee</u>-noh	the bowel; intestine; gut
el hígado	ehl <u>ee</u>-gah-doh	the liver
el riñón	ehl ree-<u>nyohn</u>	the kidney
Arm and Hand Words		
el brazo	ehl <u>bvrah</u>-soh	the arm
el antebrazo	ehl ahn-teh-<u>bvrah</u>-soh	the forearm
la muñeca	lah moo-<u>nyeh</u>-kah	the wrist
la mano	lah <u>mah</u>-noh	the hand
el dedo	ehl <u>deh</u>-doh	the finger
el pulgar	ehl pool-<u>gahr</u>	the thumb
el dedo índice	ehl <u>deh</u>-doh <u>een</u>-dee-seh	the forefinger
el dedo del medio	ehl <u>deh</u>-doh dehl <u>meh</u>-deeoh	the middle finger

Spanish	Pronunciation	English
el dedo anular	ehl <u>deh</u>-doh ah-noo-<u>lahr</u>	the ring finger
el dedo meñique	ehl <u>deh</u>-doh meh-<u>nyee</u>-keh	the little finger

Leg and Foot Words

el muslo	ehl <u>moos</u>-loh	the thigh
la pierna	lah pee<u>ehr</u>-nah	the leg
el pie	ehl pee<u>eh</u>	the foot
el dedo del pie	ehl <u>deh</u>-doh dehl pee<u>eh</u>	the toe
el tobillo	ehl toh-<u>bvee</u>-yoh	the ankle
la pantorrilla	lah pahn-toh-<u>rree</u>-yah	the calf
la planta del pie	lah <u>plahn</u>-tah dehl pee<u>eh</u>	the sole of the foot

Talking to the doctor

After you're at the doctor's office or the hospital, you may hear some of these phrases:

- ¿**Tiene cita?** *(tee<u>eh</u>-neh <u>see</u>-tah)* (Do you have an appointment?)

- **Un momento, por favor. Tome asiento en la sala de espera.** *(oon moh-<u>mehn</u>-toh, pohr fah-<u>bvohr</u> toh-meh ah-see-<u>ehn</u>-toh ehn lah <u>sah</u>-lah deh ehs-<u>peh</u>-rah)* (One moment, please. Please take a seat in the waiting room.)

- **Vamos a sacarle rayos X.** *(<u>bvah</u>-mohs ah sah-<u>kahr</u>-leh <u>rah</u>-yohs <u>eh</u>-kees)* (We'll take an X-ray.)

- **No se mueva por favor.** *(noh seh moo<u>eh</u>-bvah pohr fah-<u>bvor</u>)* (Don't move, please.)

✔ **Aquí tiene la fractura.** *(ah-kee teeeh-neh lah frahk-too-rah)* (We have a fracture here.)

✔ **Vamos a tener que enyesar su pierna.** *(bvah-mohs ah teh-nehr keh ehn-yeh-sahr soo peeehr-nah)* (We have to put your leg in a cast.)

✔ **Le voy a dar un analgésico.** *(leh bvohy a dahr oon ah-nahl-Heh-see-koh)* (I'll give you a pain killer.)

✔ **¿Tiene mareos?** *(tee-eh-neh mah-reh-ohs)* (Do you get dizzy?)

✔ **Vamos a tenerle en observación durante dos días.** *(vah-mohs ah teh-nehr-leh ehn ohbv-sehr-bvah-seeohn doo-rahn-teh dohs deeahs)* (We'll keep you under observation for two days.)

✔ **Usted tiene la presión muy alta.** *(oos-tehd teeeh-neh lah preh-seeohn mooy ahl-ta)* (You have very high blood pressure.)

Words to Know

la cita	lah see-tah	the appointment
ver	bvehr	to see
golpear	gohl-peh-ahr	to hit; to bang
el mareo	ehl mah-reh-oh	the dizziness
la observación	lah obv-sehr-bvah-seeohn	the observation

Visiting the dentist

You may find the following phrases helpful when you go to a Spanish-speaking dentist:

✔ **Necesito un dentista.** *(neh-seh-see-toh oon dehn-tees-tah)* (I need a dentist.)

✔ **¿Me puede recomendar un dentista?** *(meh pooeh-deh reh-koh-mehn-dahr oon dehn-tees-tah)* (Can you recommend a dentist?)

✔ **Doctor, me duele el diente.** *(dohk-ohr meh dooeh-leh ehl deeehn-teh)* (Doctor, I have a toothache.)

✔ **Tiene una carie.** *(tee-eh-neh oo-nah kah-reeeh)* (You have a cavity.)

✔ **Quebré una muela.** *(keh-bvreh oo-nah mooeh-lah)* (I broke a molar.)

✔ **Le pondré anestesia.** *(leh pohn-dreh ah-nehs-teh-seeah)* (I'll give you anesthesia.)

✔ **Le taparé la carie.** *(leh tah-pah-reh lah kah-reeeh)* (I can fill the cavity.)

✔ **Le sacaré la muela.** *(leh sah-kah-reh lah mooeh-lah)* (I'll [have to] pull the molar out.)

✔ **Le pondré un puente.** *(leh-pohn-dreh oon pooehn-teh)* (I'll put in a bridge.)

✔ **Le pondré una corona.** *(leh-pohn-dreh oo-nah koh-roh-nah)* (I'll put on a crown.)

Words to Know

el diente	ehl deeehn-teh	the tooth
la muela	lah mooeh-lah	the molar
la carie	lah kah-reeeh	the cavity
el dentista	ehl dehn-tees-tah	the dentist
dolor de muelas	doh-lohr deh mooeh-lahs	toothache

Ensuring that you get your money back

If you need to visit a dentist, or any other professional, while you're traveling, be sure you get a receipt to give to your insurance carrier at home. The following phrases are useful in dealing with insurance questions:

- **¿Tiene seguro dental?** *(teeeh-neh seh-goo-roh dehn-tahl)* (Do you have dental insurance?)

- **¿Tiene seguro de salud?** *(teeeh-neh seh-goo-roh deh sah-lood)* (Do you have health insurance?)

- **¿Me puede dar un recibo para el seguro?** *(meh pooeh-deh dahr ooh reh-see-bvoh pah-rah ehl seh-goo-roh)* (Can you give me a receipt for my insurance?)

Getting Help with Legal Problems

Most people obey the laws and usually don't engage in activities that involve the police or other aspects of the legal system. But accidents happen, and you may break a law that you know nothing about. If that's the case, you need help from your consulate (if you're in a foreign country) or a lawyer to make sure that your rights are protected.

Here are a couple of questions that you may want to ask first:

- **¿Hay aquí un Consulado de Estados Unidos?** *(ahy ah-kee oon kohn-soo-lah-doh deh ehs-tah-dohs oo-nee-dohs)* (Is there an American consulate here?)

- **¿Hay un abogado que hable inglés?** *(ahy oon ah-bvoh-gah-doh keh ah-bvleh een-glehs)* (Is there a lawyer who speaks English?)

Being under arrest

Hopefully, you're never arrested, but you should at least know to call a lawyer or the consul:

- ✔ **Usted va detenido.** *(oos-tehd bvah deh-teh-nee-doh)* (You're under arrest.)

- ✔ **Está circulando ebrio.** *(ehs-tah seer-koo-lahn-doh eh-bvreeoh)* (For impaired driving.)

- ✔ **Oficial, yo no tomo alcohol.** *(oh-fee-see-ahl yoh no toh-moh ahl-koh-ohl)* (Officer, I don't drink alcohol.)

- ✔ **Vamos a la comisaría.** *(bvah-mohs ah lah koh-mee-sah-reeah)* (We're going to the police station.)

- ✔ **Creo que usted se equivoca.** *(kreoh keh oos-tehd seh eh-kee-bvoh-kah)* (I believe you are mistaken.)

- ✔ **Quiero hablar con un abogado.** *(keeeh-roh ah-bvlahr kohn oon ah-bvoh-gah-doh)* (I want to talk to a lawyer.)

- ✔ **Quiero hablar con mi cónsul.** *(keeeh-roh ah-bvlahr kohn mee kohn-sool)* (I want to talk to my consulate.)

- ✔ **Quiero hablar por teléfono.** *(keeeh-roh ah-bvlahr pohr teh-leh-foh-noh)* (I want to talk on the phone.)

Stick 'em up: Words to know when you're robbed

If someone robs you while you're in a Spanish-speaking area, you can attract the help you need by using these phrases:

- ✔ **¡Un robo!** *(oon roh-bvoh)* (A burglary!)

- ✔ **¡Un asalto!** *(oon ah-sahl-toh)* (A holdup!)

✔ **¡Atrápenlo!** *(ah-trah-pehn-loh)* (Catch him!)

✔ **¡Llamen a la policía!** *(yah-mehn ah lah poh-lee-seeah)* (Call the police!)

✔ **¡Me robó la billetera!** *(meh roh-bvoh lah bvee-yeh-teh-rah)* ([She/he] stole my wallet!)

✔ **Haga una denuncia a la policía.** *(ah-gah oo-nah deh-noon-seeah ah la poh-lee-seeah)* (Report it to the police. [Literally: Make an accusation to the police.])

Reporting to the police

If you do have an unpleasant encounter with a thief, here are some words that can be helpful in describing the culprit to the police:

✔ **Era un hombre bajo, corpulento.** *(eh-rah oon ohm-bvreh bvah-Hoh kohr-poo-lehn-toh)* (He was a short man, heavyset.)

✔ **Tenía cabello oscuro y barba.** *(teh-neeah kah-bveh-yoh ohs-koo-roh ee bvahr-bvah)* (He had dark hair and a beard.)

✔ **Vestía pantalón de mezclilla, y camisa blanca.** *(bvehs-teeah pahn-tah-lohn deh mehs-klee-yah ee kah-mee-sah bvlahn-kah)* (He wore jeans, and a white shirt.)

✔ **Tendrá unos cuarenta años.** *(tehn-drah oo-nohs kooah-rehn-tah ah-nyos)* (He's around forty.)

✔ **Iba con una mujer delgada.** *(ee-bvah kohn oo-nah moo-Hehr dehl-gah-dah)* (He was with a thin woman.)

✔ **Era alta, rubia, de ojos claros.** *(eh-rah ahl-tah roo-bveeah deh oh-Hohs klah-rohs)* (She was tall, blond, light colored eyes.)

Words to Know

atacar	ah-tah-<u>kahr</u>	to attack
robar	roh-<u>bvahr</u>	to steal; to rob
oscuro	ohs-<u>koo</u>-roh	dark
claro	<u>klah</u>-roh	light
la billetera	lah bvee-yeh-<u>teh</u>-rah	the wallet
la tarjeta de crédito	lah tahr-<u>Heh</u>-tah deh <u>kreh</u>-dee-toh	the credit card
la denuncia	lah deh-<u>noon</u>-seeah	the report

Dealing with Car Emergencies

If you get in a collision, the following phrases can get you through it:

- ✔ **Hubo un choque.** (<u>oo</u>-bvoh oon <u>choh</u>-keh) (There was a collision.)

- ✔ **Paré porque cambió la luz.** (pah-<u>reh</u> pohr-<u>keh</u> kahm-bvee<u>oh</u> lah loos) (I stopped because the light changed.)

- ✔ **¿A qué velocidad iba?** (ah keh bveh-loh-see-<u>dahd</u> <u>ee</u>-bvah) (How fast were you going?)

- ✔ **Iba lento, a menos de cuarenta kilómetros.** (<u>ee</u>-bvah <u>lehn</u>-toh ah <u>meh</u>-nohs deh kooah-<u>rehn</u>-tah kee-<u>loh</u>-meh-trohs) (I was going slowly, less than 40 kilometers.)

✔ **¿Tiene usted seguro para el auto?** *(teeeh-neh oos-tehd seh-goo-roh pah-rah ehl ahoo-toh)* (Do you have car insurance?)

✔ **Sí, quiero avisar a mi compañía de seguros.** *(see, keeeh-roh ah-bvee-sahr ah mee kohm-pah-nyeeah deh seh-goo-rohs)* (Yes, I want to notify my insurance company.)

Words to Know

el choque	ehl choh-keh	the crash
la velocidad	lah-bveh-loh-see-dahd	the speed
despacio	dehs-pah-seeoh	slow
rápido	rah-pee-doh	fast
romper	rohm-pehr	to break

If your car has mechanical problems, use these phrases to find a mechanic:

✔ **Necesito ayuda. Mi auto no funciona.** *(neh-seh-see-toh ah-yoo-dah mee ahoo-toh noh foon-seeoh-nah)* (I need help. My car doesn't work.)

✔ **Buscamos un mecánico.** *(bvoos-kah-mohs oon meh-kah-nee-koh)* (We're looking for a mechanic.)

✔ **Ahora no parte.** *(ah-oh-rah noh pahr-teh)* (It won't start now.)

✔ **Vamos a revisar la batería y las bujías también.** *(bvah-mohs ah reh-bvee-sahr lah bvah-teh-reeah ee lahs bvoo-Heeahs tahm-bveeehn)* (We'll check the battery and the spark plugs, too.)

Words to Know

el mecánico	ehl meh-<u>kah</u>-nee-koh	the mechanic
partir	pahr-<u>teer</u>	to start
el motor	ehl moh-<u>tohr</u>	the engine
revisar	reh-bvee-<u>sahr</u>	to check
la batería	lah bvah-teh-<u>ree</u>ah	the battery
las bujías	lah bvoo-<u>Hee</u>ahs	the spark plugs

Chapter 12

Favorite Spanish Expressions

● ●

*T*his chapter gives you almost a dozen phrases or words that Spanish speakers use all the time in the way they greet and deal with each other.

¿Qué tal?

You use the greeting **"¿Qué tal?"** *(keh tahl)* (How are things?) when meeting someone you already know. This phrase is easy to pronounce and immediately gives the impression of someone speaking the language fluently.

¿Quiubo?

"¿Quiubo?" *(keeoo-bvoh?)* (What's up?) is very similar in its effect to **"¿Qué tal?"**, but it's even more colloquial. You use this phrase, which is common in Chile and a few other countries, only with someone you know well and with whom you have an informal relationship.

"¿Quiubo?" is a compression of the phrase **"¿qué hubo?"** *(keh oo-bvoh)*, meaning "What happened?" To really sound like an insider, let **"¿Quiubo?"** just flow out of your mouth, as though you were saying queue-boh.

¿Qué pasó?

In Mexico, you frequently hear **"¿Qué pasó?"** *(keh pah-soh)* (What's up? [Literally: What happened?])

This phrase may seem funny to you at first. Someone sees another person and cries out **"¿Qué pasó?"** as though they've been separated just before some big event and now want to know what happened. That's what the phrase means, but Spanish-speakers use it much more broadly.

Even people who barely know each other and haven't seen one another for ages can use this greeting. In any case, when you use it in Mexico, do so with someone you've seen at least once before. You'll sound like you've been there forever.

¿Cómo van las cosas?

Well-educated people use the very gentle **"¿Cómo van las cosas?"** *(koh-moh bvahn lahs koh-sahs)* (How are things going?) to express concern. People also use this phrase in cases where they've met the other person before.

"¿Cómo van las cosas?" is more appropriate than **"¿Quiubo?"** or **"¿Qué pasó?"** when greeting someone who is older than you or someone to whom you want to show your respect.

¡Del uno!

"¡Del uno!" *(dehl oo-noh)* (First rate!). This phrase is common in Chile, but you may also hear it in other places. Its meaning is clear, even if you haven't heard it before. A little ditty goes with this expression:

"¿Cómo estamos?," dijo Ramos. *(koh-moh ehs-tah-mohs dee-Hoh rah-mohs)*("How are things? [Literally: How are we?]" said Ramos.)

"**¡Del uno!**," **dijo Aceituno.** (*dehl* <u>oo</u>-*noh* <u>dee</u>-*Hoh ah-sehee-<u>too</u>-noh*) ("First rate!" said Aceituno.)

Ramos and Aceituno are just family names used to call out the rhyme. You'll sound like one of the bunch with this one.

¿Cuánto cuesta?

You ask, "**¿Cuánto cuesta?**" (*koo<u>ahn</u>-toh koo<u>ehs</u>-tah*) (How much does it cost?) when you're shopping and need to know the price.

¿A cuánto?

"**¿A cuánto?**" (*ah-koo<u>ahn</u>-toh*) (How much?) is very similar to "**¿Cuánto cuesta?**" except that this phrase may imply that you're asking the price of several things grouped together, as in "**¿A cuánto la docena?**" (*ah-koo<u>ahn</u>-toh lah doh-<u>seh</u>-nah*) (How much for the dozen?). You'll seem like an expert shopper when you use this one.

¡Un asalto!

You may think that exclaiming "**¡Un asalto!**" (*oon ah-<u>sahl</u>-toh*) (A holdup!) in the midst of bargaining for a lower price is hyping things up a bit. However, adding hype to your speech can be useful — at least the vendor knows that you're familiar with this phrase that shows your indignation.

¡Una ganga!

Vendors often use the phrase "**¡Una ganga!**" (*<u>oo</u>-nah <u>gahn</u>-gah*) (A bargain!) when trying to sell you an item. You can show your familiarity with the language when you use this expression to boast about a really good buy.

¡Buen provecho!

¡Buen provecho! *(bvooehn proh-bveh-choh)* ("Enjoy your meal!" or "Bon appetit!" [Literally: Good profit!])

Imagine that you're sitting at the table, soupspoon in hand, ready to begin your meal and about to dip it into a cup of steaming soup. In order to sound like a native, you want to say — at this exact moment — **"¡Buen provecho!"** before someone else does.

"¡Buen provecho!" is also the right thing to say when you set a tray of food in front of your guests.

¡Salud!

"¡Salud!" *(sah-lood)* (Health!) has two usages:

- You use this word when giving a toast as a way to say "Cheers!"

- You use this word after someone sneezes — it's the Spanish equivalent of "Bless you," to which you answer, **"¡Gracias!"**

¡Buen viaje!

You hear the phrase **"¡Buen viaje!"** *(bvooehn bveeah-Heh)* (Have a good trip!) all around you in train stations, airports, and bus terminals. Use this expression when you want to wish those you care for a safe trip.

If you're reading this book as part of your preparation for travel, then we want to say **"¡Buen viaje!"** to you.

Chapter 13

Phrases That Make You Sound Like a Local

● ●

Knowing just a few words — as long as they're the right words — can convince others that you speak Spanish fluently. Certain phrases can make a big difference, too. This chapter gives you not quite ten Spanish phrases to use at the right moments, in the right places. You can impress your friends and have fun, too.

¡Esta es la mía!

The exclamation **¡Esta es la mía!** *(<u>ehs</u>-tah ehs lah <u>meeah</u>)* (This is my chance! [Literally: This one is mine!]) is a natural when you see an opportunity and go for it.

In this phrase, **la** *(lah)* (the) refers to **una oportunidad** *(oo-nah oh-pohr-too-nee-<u>dahd</u>)* (an opportunity), but you can use it in the sense of "I have it!" as well. For instance, you may be fishing, waiting for **el pez** *(ehl pehs)* (the fish). The instant the fish bites, yelling **¡Este es el mío!** is appropriate. You use the same phrase when you're waiting to catch **un vuelo** *(oon <u>bvooeh</u>-loh)* (a flight) or **un bus** *(oon bvoos)* (a bus). When you see your plane or bus arrive, you say, **¡Este es el mío!**

¿Y eso con qué se come?

¿Y eso con qué se come? *(ee eh-soh kohn keh seh koh-meh)* (What on earth is that? [Literally: And what do you eat that with?]) is a fun phrase that implies considerable knowledge of the language. The phrase is quite classical, and doesn't belong to one country or another. You say, **"¿Y eso con qué se come?"** when you run across something absurd or unknown.

Voy a ir de farra

When you're getting ready for a night on the town, you'll sound like a native if you say, **"¡Voy a ir de farra!"** *(bvohy ah eer deh fah-rrah)* (I'm going to party!) You frequently hear the word **farra** *(fah-rrah)* (partying; good time) in South America. This word even has a verb form: **farrear** *(fah-rreh-ahr)* (to party; to have a good time).

Caer fatal

You use the verb phrase **Caer fatal a uno** *(kah-ehr fah-tahl ah oo-noh)* (to strongly dislike something) to say that something unpleasant has happened to you. You can use **caer fatal** for almost anything that you don't like or that hurts you in some way. For example,

✔ You can say, **"Sus bromas me caen fatal"** *(soos bvroh-mahs meh kah-ehn fah-tahl)* (I can't stand her/his jokes) when someone's sense of humor really gets on your nerves.

✔ You can say, **"La comida me cayó fatal"** *(lah koh-mee-dah meh kah-yoh fah-tahl)* (The food made me sick) when suffering some painful consequence of eating food that didn't agree with you.

Nos divertimos en grande

The phrase **nos divertimos en grande** *(nohs dee-bvehr-tee-mohs ehn grahn-deh)* means "We had a great time." You can use **en grande** *(ehn grahn-deh)* (a lot; much; greatly; in a big way) for many things. For instance, you can say, **"Comimos en grande"** *(koh-mee-mohs ehn grahn-deh)* (We ate tremendously) after a feast, or **"Gozamos en grande"** *(goh-sah-mohs ehn gran-deh)* (We really, really enjoyed ourselves) after an extraordinarily pleasant event.

Ver negro para

The idiom **ver negro para . . .** *(bvehr neh-groh pah-rah)* (to have a hard time of . . . [Literally: to see black to . . .]) followed by a verb beautifully conveys that a task is hugely difficult. The following list gives you some examples of this phrase in action:

> ✔ **Las vimos negras para terminarlo.** *(lahs bvee-mohs neh-grahs pah-rah tehr-mee-nahr-loh)* (We had a hard time finishing it.)

> ✔ **Los refugiados se las vieron negras para salir del área.** *(lohs reh-foo-Heeah-dohs seh lahs bvee-eh-rohn neh-grahs pah-rah sah-leer dehl ah-reh-ah)* (The refugees had a hard time leaving the area.)

Pasó sin pena ni gloria

You generally use the phrase **pasó sin pena ni gloria** *(pah-soh seen peh-nah nee gloh-reeah)* (it was neither here nor there) to talk about an event that had little echo with you or the public. Following are some examples of how you may use this phrase:

> ✔ **El concierto pasó sin pena ni gloria.** *(ehl kohn-see-ehr-toh pah-soh seen peh-nah nee gloh-reeah)* (The concert was neither here nor there.)

- **La reunión pasó sin pena ni gloria.** *(lah rehoo-neeohn pah-soh seen peh-nah nee gloh-reeah)* (The meeting was neither here nor there.)

- **La cena se acabó sin pena ni gloria.** *(lah seh-nah seh ah-kah-bvoh seen peh-nah nee gloh-reeah)* (The supper was eaten, but it was just so-so.)

¡Así a secas!

¡Así a secas! *(ah-see ah seh-kahs)* (Just like that!) is an idiom that conveys astonishment or disbelief. You can use this phrase in many ways — often with a snap of your fingers to help show just how quickly something happened. For instance, if you happen to know someone who always seems to be borrowing your money, you may say something like **"Me pidió mil dólares, ¡así a secas!"** *(meh pee-deeoh meel doh-lah-rehs ah-see ah seh-kahs)* (He asked me for a thousand dollars, just like that!)

¡La cosa va viento en popa!

The idiom **¡La cosa va viento en popa!** *(lah koh-sah bvah bvee-ehn-toh ehn poh-pah)* (It's going exceedingly well! [Literally: It's moving with the wind from the stern!]) comes from the language of sailing. The race is on, and the wind is coming into the sail from the stern — nothing could go faster or better. You may also say the following:

- **¡El trabajo anduvo viento en popa!** *(ehl trah-bvah-Hoh anh-doo-bvoh bveeehn-toh ehn poh-pah)* (The job went exceedingly well!)

- **El partido salió viento en popa!** *(ehl pahr-tee-doh sah-leeoh bveeehn-toh ehn poh-pah)* (The game went exceedingly well!)

- **El aprendizaje del español va viento en popa!** *(ehl ah-prehn-dee-sah-Heh dehl ehs-pah-nyohl bvah bveeehn-toh ehn poh-pah)* (Learning Spanish is going exceedingly well!)

Index

Notes

Notes

....

_____

_____

_____

_____

_____

_____

_____

_____

_____

_____

_____

_____

_____

_____

_____

_____

_____